Ruby Quick Syntax Reference

Matt Clements

Apress®

Ruby Quick Syntax Reference

ISBN-13 (pbk): 978-1-4302-6568-9

ISBN-13 (electronic): 978-1-4302-6569-6

Managing Director: Welmoed Spahr
Lead Editor: Louise Corrigan
Technical Reviewer: Magesh S
Editorial Board: Steve Anglin, Mark Beckner, Ewan Buckingham, Gary Cornell, Louise Corrigan, Jim DeWolf, Jonathan Gennick, Robert Hutchinson, Michelle Lowman, James Markham, Matthew Moodie, Jeff Olson, Jeffrey Pepper, Douglas Pundick, Ben Renow-Clarke, Dominic Shakeshaft, Gwenan Spearing, Matt Wade, Steve Weiss
Coordinating Editor: Christine Ricketts
Copy Editor: Linda Seifert
Compositor: SPi Global
Indexer: SPi Global
Artist: SPi Global
Cover Designer: Anna Ishchenko

Distributed to the book trade worldwide by Springer Science+Business Media New York, 233 Spring Street, 6th Floor, New York, NY 10013. Phone 1-800-SPRINGER, fax (201) 348-4505, e-mail orders-ny@springer-sbm.com, or visit www.springeronline.com. Apress Media, LLC is a California LLC and the sole member (owner) is Springer Science + Business Media Finance Inc (SSBM Finance Inc). SSBM Finance Inc is a **Delaware** corporation.

For information on translations, please e-mail rights@apress.com, or visit www.apress.com.

Apress and friends of ED books may be purchased in bulk for academic, corporate, or promotional use. eBook versions and licenses are also available for most titles. For more information, reference our Special Bulk Sales–eBook Licensing web page at www.apress.com/bulk-sales.

Any source code or other supplementary materials referenced by the author in this text is available to readers at www.apress.com. For detailed information about how to locate your book's source code, go to www.apress.com/source-code/.

For Sarah, Jacob & Samuel.

Contents at a Glance

Contents

About the Author

Matt Clements is an experienced Developer, building Web & Native applications over the last 8 years. Working in the Finance Industry for a Direct Debit Collection Company DFC (http://www.debitfinance.co.uk/) as the IT Development Manager, Matt manages a team of Developers across a number of technologies. Matt also works as a Freelance Developer building Web Applications for numerous clients.

He lives in Milton Keynes, with his wife Sarah, two boys Jacob and Samuel, and black Labrador Ember.

About the Technical Reviewer

Magesh S is a partner at Hash14, a software company that offers both consulting and training. He has worked for several startups and SME's in Chennai, which adds up to 5+ years of technical and corporate experience. He is passionate about technology, Ruby and Open source software. He enjoys blogging, tweeting and socializing at tech and startup events.

Acknowledgments

Firstly I would like to lend my thanks to the Apress Team, without who this book wouldn't have been possible. My Coordinating Editor, Christine Ricketts who's encouragement, and support throughout the process has been invaluable. Thanks to the technical reviewer Magesh, who's ongoing reviews and ideas have enhanced this book at every chapter. Also, thanks to my Lead Editor, Louise Corrigan who initially gave me the chance to write this book; and who's constant patience and support has allowed me to complete this book. My final thanks to the whole Apress Team, who have brought this initially concept to publication.

Massive thanks are deserved for my family and friends, who have supported me throughout the process of my writing this book. Thanks to my wife Sarah and two son's Jacob & Samuel who have encouraged, and supported me at every stage of the process. Further thanks to my Mum, Dad and Brother Michael for their boosted help during this process.

I owe thanks to my work colleagues for massive patience whilst I have been writing the book, and for offering me their views, reviews, and encouragement on a day-to-day basis.

My final thanks go out of the Ruby community, who have offered endless resources and support to what I am writing; who have openly shared examples of their work, ideas of applications, and provided support during any pitfalls in order to assist me during my programming work. Likewise to all of the web community, and I hope you enjoy!

Introduction

Welcome to *Ruby Quick Syntax Reference* and thank you for purchasing and reading this book. During this book we will investigate and discover the basics of the Ruby programming language, along with discovering the syntax used, the way that the Ruby programming language works, and overcoming any pitfalls or caveats with the Ruby language.

Ruby is a powerful and easily language to discover and learn, if you don't know how to program Ruby is a very simple language to pick up and learn; but if you have programmed previously, such as in PHP, Perl, Pascal or C you will find Ruby an easy language to grasp.

Ruby is a very pragmatic language, often having multiple ways of doing things; I will highlight within the book the options available to you as a programmer, along with any pitfalls to avoid.

We won't cover any bloated samples, or drawn out history lessons; but instead quick details as to what we can achieve with the Ruby language, and quick syntax notes as to how to write Ruby code. This book has been written to learn from scratch, with very little previous experience programming; or as a quick syntax guide to pick up and remind you of the syntax and abilities of the Ruby language.

Ruby was designed and developed by Yukihiro "Matz"Matsumoto in the mid-90's, but is now used across the world, and often is commonly known when used within the framework Rails (Ruby on Rails), but can also be used on it's own, or with other frameworks. Ruby is used by sites such as Twitter, Shopify, Airbnb and Github.

I hope you enjoy the book, and see you in Chapter 1.

CHAPTER 1

■ ■ ■

Introducing Ruby

Ruby is a dynamic, object-oriented, programming language with an expressive syntax. It takes inspiration from several languages such as *Smalltalk*, *Lisp*, and *Perl*, adding features that make it very pleasant to program with. In recent years, Ruby exploded in popularity mainly thanks to the success of web development frameworks such as *Ruby on Rails* and *Sinatra*. However, it is also used with success in many other different contexts such as computer security (*Metasploit*), voice communications (A*dhearsion*), and server configuration (*Opscode Chef* and *Puppet*), to name just a few.

Installing Ruby

In this book, we use the latest stable version available, which is, at the time of writing, the *2.0.0-p247*. If you are using a Linux distribution or Mac OS X, you'll find a Ruby interpreter already installed. However, it might be an outdated version and usually it also has some limitations caused by the package manager on your operating system (for example, apt for Debian/Ubuntu linux distributions).

There are several ways to install the latest version of the Ruby interpreter, depending on the operating system you are using. If you already have this version installed, feel free to skip the following section.

Installing on Linux or Mac OS X

Even if Linux and Mac OS X are completely different operating systems, they both share the same UNIX philosophy and tools under the hood, so we have grouped them in the same section.

It is usually a good idea to install Ruby from source as this gives you more control over the installed version and, sometimes, lets you customize the installation. However, instead of manually downloading and compiling the Ruby source code, we are going to to use a tool called *Ruby Version Manager* (https://rvm.io) that helps you to easily install, manage, and work with multiple Ruby environments and interpreters. This means that, in theory, you can use several versions installed. Before you can install RVM and Ruby you need to install some dependencies. These can be development tools such as the compiler, or just external libraries like OpenSSL.

Linux Dependencies

On Debian/Ubuntu Linux, you can install these dependencies using the following command inside a terminal:

```
sudo apt-get install build-essential openssl libreadline6 libreadline6-
dev curl git-core zlib1g zlib1g-dev libssl-dev libyaml-dev libsqlite3-dev
sqlite3 libxml2-dev libxslt-dev autoconf libc6-dev ncurses-dev automake
libtool bison subversion pkg-config libgdbm-dev libffi-dev libreadline-dev
```

Some of the preceding packages are already installed because they are pretty common dependencies. This is not a problem; the apt tool manages this for you automatically.

If you are using another Linux distribution (Fedora/RedHat/CentOS, Arch Linux, etc.), don't worry, they all have a package management system that will help you install the dependencies.

Mac OS X Dependencies

On Mac OS X there isn't a default package manager; however, most people use Homebrew (http://brew.sh) and so do we. To do this, you need to have Xcode installed along with its command line tools. If you don't have Xcode installed, we suggest you install it from the Apple Mac App Store and install the command line tools in Xcode Preferences (Figure 1-1)

Figure 1-1. *Command line tools*

Once Xcode and its command line tools are installed, you can proceed with the Homebrew installation. As we mentioned previously, Mac OS X ships with its default Ruby, we are going to use it to bootstrap Homebrew, which is written in Ruby too. Open Term.app and run the following command:

```
ruby -e "$(curl -fsSL https://raw.github.com/mxcl/homebrew/go)"
```

To check whether all the process went correctly, run:

```
brew doctor
```

This checks whether your system has all the tools and settings to run Homebrew properly. For example, you might be faced with this error:

```
Error: No such file or directory - /usr/local/Cellar
```

Don't worry, it's just telling you that the default directory used by Homebrew to store all its stuff is missing. You can fix this with the following commands:

```
sudo mkdir /usr/local/Cellar
sudo chown -R `whoami` /usr/local
```

Setting Up RVM

Now that you have the tools for compiling and installing programs from source, you can finally install RVM. For now it doesn't matter if you are on Linux or Mac OS X, in both cases you have all the requirements. Run the following command inside your shell:

```
curl -L get.rvm.io | bash
```

This command installs and sets up RVM tools in your user directory, which means that RVM is available only for your current user and all the files are installed under your home directory. Once the installation is complete, you need two more steps. Run the following command to use RVM in the current shell:

```
source ~/.rvm/scripts/rvm
```

Add the following line to your ~/.profile to load RVM every time you open your terminal:

```
[[ -s "$HOME/.rvm/scripts/rvm" ]] && source "$HOME/.rvm/scripts/rvm"
```

As we have already seen for Homebrew, even RVM has a tool to check that all its requirements are met. Run the following command:

```
rvm requirements
```

If you have any missing required packages, you will need to install them before continuing by running `brew install <missing package name>` or `apt-get install <missing package name>`.

Installing Ruby 2.0.0

As stated before, RVM lets you install and use different Ruby versions on your system with ease. However, for our purposes, we are going to install only the latest stable available release. In your terminal, run the following command:

```
rvm install 2.0.0-p247
```

Now RVM downloads, compiles, and installs the specified version. Once it finishes, you need to set it as default Ruby interpreter and check that it works:

```
rvm use 2.0.0-p247 --default
ruby -v
```

The output may vary depending on the operating system you are using; however it should look something like this:

```
ruby 2.0.0p247 (2013-06-27 revision 41674) [x86_64-darwin12.4.0]
```

Installing on Windows

On Windows things are bit different. Download the official installer on `http://rubyinstaller.org/downloads/`, then run it and you're done.

A Quick Tour

Now we are ready for a quick tour of Ruby–just to get your feet wet. Don't worry if something is not clear at first glance, the code snippets shown here are just for demonstration, each detail will be explained in later chapters of this book.

irb: The Interactive Ruby Shell

Before starting with examples, we'll introduce *irb* (short for *interactive Ruby*), a Ruby shell. In other words, you type a Ruby expression at the irb prompt, and the expression will be evaluated and displayed. In this way, you can quickly try out small snippets without the need to edit a file and the run it. Open a terminal and run `irb`:

```
irb(main):001:0> 1 + 1
=> 2
irb(main):002:0> 'hello ' * 3
=> 'hello hello hello'
```

Type **exit** to close `irb`.

Object-Oriented

If you are not new to programming, you might have already heard of object-oriented languages such as Java or C#. However, Ruby is a bit different: it is *completely* object-oriented. In Ruby every value is an *object*, even numbers and booleans. In the following examples, you can see how a method is called on basic objects such as a numeric literal and a string. The # character indicates a comment (anything after it is not executed) and => is a commonly used convention to indicate the value returned by the commented code.

```
1.odd? # => true
1.even? # => false
'hello'.reverse # => 'olleh'
'hello'.length # => 5
```

Also note how parentheses are omitted–they are optional and make the code more readable. We'll see several, more focused examples in the next chapters.

Blocks and Iterators

There are methods called *iterators* that act as loops. They take a piece of code called a *block* to serve as the body of the loop and to be executed at each iteration. Here are some simple examples:

```
1.upto(5) {|n| puts n } # Prints '12345'
a = [1, 2, 3] # Create an array literal
a.each do |n| # Multiline block call
  print n * 2 # Prints '246'
end
a.map {|n| n * 2} # => [2, 4, 6]
```

Although blocks are mainly used for loop-like constructs, it is also possible for methods that invoke the block only once:

```
File.open('example.txt') do |f| # Open the file and pass the stream to block
  print f.readline # Read from the file
end # Close the stream when the block ends
```

Modules

Modules define a namespace, a sandbox that groups together methods, classes, and constants and can be included in classes to extend their behavior. For example:

```
module Greeter # Define a module called Greeter
  def greet # Define a method called 'greet'
    puts "Hello!"
  end
end

class Person # Define a class called Person
  include Greeter # Include the Greeter module
end

alice = Person.new # Instantiate a new Person
alice.greet # Call the method 'greet' from the instance
```

Again, this is just a simple introduction; we'll discuss this more in the chapters that follow.

Duck Typing

Unlike other object-oriented languages, the *type* of an object is defined more by its methods and attributes rather than from its *class*. This is called *duck typing* because of the motto:

If it walks like a duck and talks like a duck, then I treat it like a duck

There is no need to define an object as a certain type as in most other object-oriented languages. This makes the syntax easy for new developers using Ruby for the first time.
Let's use a simple example to show how it works:

```
# define a simple method that accepts any object with a 'each' method
def duck_printer(object)
  if object.respond_to? :each # check if object has a method called 'each'
    object.each {|n| print n } # iterates over the contents and print them
  else # otherwise raise an error
    raise "passed argument doesn't provide #each method."
  end
end
```

```
# define some variables with different classes
hash = {a: 1, b: 2, c: 3}
array = [1, 2, 3]
string = 'hello'

# with an Hash
duck_printer hash # Prints '[:a, 1][:b, 2][:c, 3]'

# with an Array
duck_printer array # Prints '123'

# with a String
duck_printer string # Raises a RuntimeError with our error message
```

Where to Find Ruby Documentation

There are a lot of resources to dive in to the Ruby documentation, both on Internet and on your own computer as well.

RDoc and ri

Like many other languages, Ruby has adopted an internal documentation system called *RDoc*. This documentation can be extracted from its source and exported to HTML or *ri* formats. The *ri* tool is a local documentation viewer that can be invoked from your terminal. For example, if you want to find documentation for the Hash class, just type:

```
ri Hash
```

To exit, type **q**. You can also get information on a particular method by passing its name as a parameter:

```
ri Hash.merge
ri Hash#each
```

If the method you pass to ri occurs in more than one *class* or *module*, then it shows all the implementations on the same page. Finally, you can search and read documentation online at http://ruby-doc.org, just be sure to choose the correct Ruby documentation for your installed version.

CHAPTER 2

▓ ▓ ▓

Operators

Expressions

Unlike other programming languages, in Ruby there isn't a distinction between statements and expressions: everything is evaluated as an expression that produces a return value. The simplest expressions are:

- *literals*: values such as numbers, strings, arrays, hashes, etc...

- *variable and constant references*: A variable (or a constant) is referenced by citing its name. For example:

  ```
  x = 1 # assignment expression
  x # variable reference expression
  MY_CONST # constant reference
  ```

- *method invocations*: the (return) value of a method invocation is the value of the last evaluated expression in the body of the method.

Operators

Expressions can be combined through *operators*. An *operator* represents an operation (such as addition, multiplication or even a comparison) that is performed on one or more values, called *operands*, to build another, bigger, expression. For example, we can take two numeric literals such as **2** and **3**, then use the **+** operator to combine them and produce the value **5**. There are three characteristics you need to know about operators to use them in proper way: *arity*, *precedence* and *associativity*.

The *arity* of an operator is the number of operands it operates on. For example binary operators expect two operands, while the unary operators expect only one.

The *precedence* of an operator affects the order of evaluation of an expression. For example:

```
1 + 2 * 2 # => 5
```

As you can see, the addition operator has a lower precedence than the multiplication operator, that's why the above expression evaluates to **5** and not **6**. However, you are free to change the default order of precedence by grouping specific sub expressions inside parentheses. Here is how we can obtain a different result by modifying the above example:

```
(1 + 2) * 2 # => 6
```

We have grouped the two addition operands so that the expression inside the parentheses would be evaluated as a whole value before it becomes another operand for the multiplication.

The *associativity* of an operator specifies the order of evaluation when the same operator (or operators with the same precedence) appears sequentially in an expression. Each operator has a different order to evaluate an expression: left to right, right to left and the case where an operator is not associative, so that you need to use parentheses to determine the desired evaluation order.

As you may already know, most arithmetic operators are left-associative, which means that **2 + 2 - 3** is evaluated as **(2 + 2) - 3** rather than **2 + (2 - 3)**. On the other end, exponentiation is right-associative, so **2**3**4** is evaluated as **2**(3**4)**.

Several Ruby operators are implemented as methods, allowing classes (or even single objects) to define new meanings for those operators. For example, the **String** class implements the **+** operator to concatenate two strings. Table 2-1 at the end of the chapter, shows a list of the main Ruby operators, ordered by higher to lower precedence.

At the end of this chapter, you'll find a table to summarize all the operators, meanwhile, we'll explain some of them in the next pages.

Arithmetic: + - * / %

The arithmetic operators perform on all **Numeric** classes, this is a very common behavior in other programming languages. Other classes, might use some of these operators to perform other operations. For example, the **String** class uses the **+** operator to concatenate two strings and the ***** operator is used to repeat it, while **Array** uses **+** and **-** operator to respectively perform array concatenation and array subtraction.

```
1 + 1 # => 2
5 / 2 # => 2
5 % 2 # => 1
"hello" + "world" # => "hello world"
"hello" * 3 # => "hello hello hello"
2 / 0 # => ZeroDivisionError
2.0 / 0 # => NaN
[1, 2] + [3, 4] # => [1, 2, 3, 4]
[1, 2] - [1] # => [2]
```

Shift or Append: << >>

As we have already seen with arithmetic operators, the **<<** and **>>** operators can behave differently, depending by the classes they are operating on. The **Fixnum** and **Bignum** classes, define the **<<** and **>>** operators to shift the bits of the left-hand respectively to the left and to the right.

```
10 << 1 # => 20
10 >> 1 # => 5
```

On the other hand, the **<<** operator is used by **String, Array, IO** and many other classes as an append operator:

```
"hello" << "world" # => "hello world"
"hello" << "appended " << "world" # => "hello appended world"
[] << 1 # => [1]
[] << 1 << 2 # => [1, 2]
STDOUT << "hello" # prints "hello" to standard output stream
```

Comparison: < <= > >= <=>

The comparison operators are used to make assertions about the relative order of two values. Usually, some classes are ordered by their values: numbers are ordered by magnitude, strings are ordered alphabetically and dates are ordered chronologically.

```
2 > 1 # => true

"hello" > "a" #=> true
"hello" > "z" #=> false

now = Time.now
sleep 5
later = Time.now
now > later # => false
```

However, classes may define their own comparison operators individually or, more commonly, by defining the **<=>** operator which is a general purpose comparison operator that returns the relative order of two values: it is **-1** if the left-hand value is less than the right-hand operand, **+1** if the left-hand is greater than the right-hand, and **0** if they are equal. The operator **<=>** alone, doesn't come too much in handy, but when you define it and include the **Comparable** module inside a class, then you'll get the other comparison operators such as **>** **<**, ==, and **>=** **<=**. Here is a simple example:

```
class Person
  include Comparable
  attr_reader :name

  def initialize(name)
    @name = name
  end
```

```
  # define the comparison operator by using the 'name' attribute
  def <=> other
    self.name <=> other.name
  end
end

mario = Person.new 'Mario'
luigi = Person.new 'Luigi'

mario > luigi # => true
```

As you can see, in this case the comparison is based on the **Person**'s **name** attribute (a **String** value), however, we can change its behavior by considering another field or attribute, such as **age** (**Numeric**) or **birthday** (**Time**, **Date** or similar).

Booleans: && ‖ ! and or not

Boolean operators are built into the Ruby language and are not based on methods like we've seen with comparison operators. This means, for example, that classes cannot define this kind of operator. Unlike many other programming languages, Ruby doesn't have boolean types, however it defines **true** or **false** special values. As a rule of thumb, the **false** and **nil** are considered false, true in all other cases. Let's see some basic example:

```
x = 5
x > 0 && x < 10 # => true AND true => true
x < 0 || x == 5 # false OR true => true
!(x > 0) # => !true => false
```

In this case, there are two comparisons which return a boolean value. However, because the non-null values of the elements are considered true, the return value of a boolean expression is either the value of the elements:

```
y = 6
z = false
x && y # => 5 AND 6 => 6
z && x # => false AND 5 => false
z || x # => false OR 5 => 5
result = !z && (x || y) # => true && (5 || 6) => 5
```

As you can see, the returned value depends by the result of the boolean expression. For example, the **&&** operator first evaluates the left-hand operand and returns that value if the expression is **nil** or **false**, otherwise it returns the value of the right-hand expression. A side advantage of this is the opportunity to execute expressions in a very succinct and declarative way. Consider the following simple example:

```
def max(x, y)
  # the righthand expression would be skipped if x is not greater than y
  x > y && return x
  return y
end
```

Beside the fact that the above method might be written in several different ways, the point here is to show how the boolean operator might skip the righthand operator in case the first expression is false.

Until now we have used the high precedence versions of the boolean operators, but there are also the low precedence ones: **and**, **or** and **not**, respectively referred to **&&**, **||** and **!**. The following example shows how this precedence gap can influence the results of two apparently similar constructs:

```
x || y && nil # => x
x or y and nil # => nil
```

Ranges: .. ...

Ranges are a very common occurrence in programming, for example when referring to time intervals (eg: from Monday to Sunday). Ruby uses ranges to implement *sequences*, *conditions* and *intervals*.

Sequences are the most common usage of ranges in Ruby. They have a start, an end point and a way to produce successive values. To do this, you need to use the range **..** operators and **...**. The first form creates an inclusive range, while the three-dot form creates a range that excludes the last value:

```
1..10 # from 1 to 10
1...10 # from 1 to 9
'a'..'Z' # all characters from 'a' to 'Z'
```

Ranges can be converted to **Array** or **Enumerator** using **to_a** or **to_enum**.

```
(1..10).to_a # => [1, 2, 3, 4, 5, 6, 7, 8, 9, 10]
alphabet = ('a'..'z').to_enum
alphabet.next # => 'a'
alphabet.next # => 'b'
```

Ranges as conditions are a bit less common in everyday Ruby programming, however it has its benefits for certain constructs. Here's a brief example that prints a set of lines from standard input where the first line in each set contains the word *start* and the last line contains *end*.

```
while line = gets
  puts line if line =~ /start/.. line =~ /end/
end
```

Ranges as intervals are more common than the use as conditions. It is possible to check if some value falls within the interval represented by a range using the **===** operator:

```
(1..10) === 5 # => true
(1..10) === 'a' # => false
('a'..'z') === 'A' # => false
```

Table 2-1. *Operators precedence, high to low precedence*

Operator	Assoc.	Method	Operation
! ~	Right	✓	Boolean NOT, bitwise complement
**	Right	✓	Exponentiation
+ -	Right	✓	Unary plus and minus
* / %	Left	✓	Multiplication, division, modulo
+ -	Left	✓	Plus and minus
<< >>	Left	✓	Bitwise shift-left and shift-right
&	Left	✓	Bitwise AND
| ^	Left	✓	Bitwise OR and XOR
< <= >= >	Left	✓	Comparison
== === != =~ !~ !~ <=>	✓	✓	Equality and pattern matching
&& and ||	Left	✓	Boolean AND and OR
.. ...	✓	✓	Range creation
?:	Left	✓	Conditional (ternary operator)
rescue	Right	✓	Exception handling modifier
= **= *= %= += -= <<= >>= &&= ||= |= ^=	Right	✓	Assignment
not and or	Left	✓	Boolean NOT, AND and OR
if unless while until	✓	✓	Expression modifiers
begin/end	✓	✓	Block expression

CHAPTER 3

■ ■ ■

Strings

String Literals

A string within Ruby is a sequence of one of more bytes, typically a set of characters. These can be created, manipulated, and output when required. Strings are generally wrapped in single or double quotation marks:

```
2.1.0 :001 > puts "Hello World"
Hello World

2.1.0 :001 > puts 'Hello World'
Hello World
```

However if the string contains another double/single quote, these will need to be escaped in order for the string to be complete, and the code to compile:

```
2.1.0 :001'> puts 'Welcome to John's website'
SyntaxError: (irb):5: syntax error, unexpected tIDENTIFIER, expecting
end-of-input
puts 'Welcome to John's website' #
                       ^
from /Users/matt/.rvm/rubies/ruby-2.1.0/bin/irb:1:in `<main>'
2.1.0 :001 > puts 'Welcome to John\'s website'
Welcome to John's website
```

Because John's contains a single quote mark, and the string is contained in single quotes, a backslash is required before the quote mark within the string for the code to compile and run.

There is one minor difference between using single and double quotes within Ruby, in regards to the supported escape characters that are permitted.

Single quotes support:

```
\' = Escaping a single quote using a backslash
\\ = Escaping a backslash with another backslash
```

Double quotes support a much broader range of escape characters as well as embedding Ruby variables and code within the string literals. The embedding of Ruby variables/code within a string literal is known as *interpolation*:

```
\" = Escaping a double quote using a backslash
\\ = Escaping a backslash with another backslash
\a = Bell/Alert
\b = Backspace
\r = Carriage Return
\n = New Line
\s = Space
\t = Tab
```

```
puts "Welcome to John's Website\nWhich page would you like to visit"
page = gets.chomp
puts "Welcome to John's #{page}!" #=> "Welcome to John's Blog!"
```

```
puts "2 + 2 = #{2+2}" #=> 2 + 2 = 4
```

```
puts "Seconds/day: #{24*60*60}" #=> Seconds/day: 86400
```

There are also three other alternatives to the single/double quotes used previously. We can use a *here document,* which is ideal for long passages of text as follows:

```
puts text = <<END
Lorem ipsum dolor sit amet, consectetur adipiscing elit
Donec at neque sapien. Donec eu libero quis erat
volutpat venenatis. Vivamus suscipit elit eu odio facilisis
END
```

```
#=> Lorem ipsum dolor sit amet, consectetur adipiscing elit
Donec at neque sapien. Donec eu libero quis erat
volutpat venenatis. Vivamus suscipit elit eu odio facilisis
```

We can also use %q and %Q start delimited strings, which allow you to specify the start delimiter and will continue until the next occurrence of the delimiter is reached.

```
%q{Hello World, Welcome to John's Website!}
%q/Hello World, Welcome to John's Website/
%q*Hello World, Welcome to John's Website*
#=> Hello World, Welcome to John's Website
```

In the previous code samples we have used the function puts, which outputs the following string, followed by a new line by default. We can also instead use the function print, which does not output a new line by default.

```
2.1.0 :001 > print "Hello", "World", "Welcome", "to", "my", "Website"
HelloWorldWelcometomyWebsite

2.1.0 :002 > puts "Hello", "World", "Welcome", "to", "my", "Website"
Hello
World
Welcome
to
my
Website
```

String Methods

A number of string manipulation methods are made available within Ruby to easily manipulate the string. Some of the most common manipulation methods are

```
"Hello John".downcase #=> "hello john"
"Hello John".upcase #=> "HELLO JOHN"
"hello john".capitalize #=> "Hello john"
"Hello John".swapcase #=> "hELLO jOHN"
"Hello John".reverse #=> "nhoJ olleH"
```

These string manipulation methods can also be used inline to manipulate a variable by appending an exclamation mark to the method:

```
hello = "Hello John"
hello.downcase!
puts hello #=> "hello john"
```

Further string methods are available within Ruby to interpret a string in a number of ways:

```
"Hello John".length #=> 10
"Hello John".empty? #=> false
"1000".to_s #=> "1000" #Cast & Output to String
"1000".to_i #=> 1000 #Cast & Output to Integer
"1000".to_f #=> 1000.0 #Cast & Output to Float
```

Concatenating Strings

Within Ruby there are a number of ways to concatenate strings together. These all have minor differences to their functionality, but more-so come down to personal preference.

```
puts "Hello " << "world" #=> "Hello world"
puts "Hello " + "world" #=> "Hello world"
```

17

```
text = "world"
puts "Hello #{text}" #=> "Hello world"
```

The main difference between the + and << concatenations are that << changes the variable on the left, where as the + does not.

```
msg = "Hello"

puts msg + "World" #this doesn't change the variable
puts msg #=> Hello

puts msg << "World" #this changes the variable
puts msg #=> World
```

Repeating Strings

We can use arithmetic to repeat strings when required. This is written by providing a String, followed by the arithmetic symbol for times *, then the number of times that the string should be repeated.

```
puts "Hello"*3 #=> "HelloHelloHello"
```

Extracting Strings

Within Ruby we have two methods to extract subsets of strings. These are substring and character extraction.

Character extraction extracts a single character from a string by providing the characters location as an integer. Note that the first position is notated as position 0:

```
puts "Hello"[1] #=> "e"
```

We can also use negative positions to output a character by position from right to left (note that the last character is notated as -1):

```
puts "Hello"[-1] #=> "o"
```

Alternatively we can output a number of characters from within a string, by using substring, rather than character extraction. We use the same notation of character positions (0 = First Character), however we supply a second parameter to show the length of the substring. This means that [0,3] would detail starting at the first character (0), and outputting 3 characters (3).

```
puts "Hello"[0,3] #=> "Hel"
```

Utilizing Strings

The Ruby String class is one of the largest Ruby classes, with over 150 methods available to utilize. We are going to interpret a text file of DVDs within a collection using String methods to output a list of available films under 125 minutes that are suitable for a 14 year old by:

```
100000  |      2:17   |   Skyfall                 |     12
100001  |      2:06   |   The Hurt Locker         |     15
100002  |      1:45   |   21 Jump Street          |     15
100003  |      1:40   |   Finding Nemo            |     U
```

To start off, we set the preceding text into a variable, loop through per line and then split each column when a vertical bar is found (with optional spaces):

```
dvds = <<EOF
100000  |      2:17   |   Skyfall                 |     12
100001  |      2:06   |   The Hurt Locker         |     15
100002  |      1:45   |   21 Jump Street          |     15
100003  |      1:40   |   Finding Nemo            |     U
EOF

dvds.chomp.split(/\n/).each do |line|
  id, length, name, rating = line.chomp.split(/\s*\|\s*/)
  puts name
end

#=>
Skyfall
The Hurt Locker
21 Jump Street
Finding Nemo
```

We now need to calculate from this list the suitable films for the 14 year old to watch. We use some simple if statements utilizing string comparisons/methods to output the suitable films.

```
dvds = <<EOF
100000  |      2:17   |   Skyfall                 |     12
100001  |      2:06   |   The Hurt Locker         |     15
100002  |      1:45   |   21 Jump Street          |     15
100003  |      1:40   |   Finding Nemo            |     U
EOF
```

```
dvds.chomp.split(/\n/).each do |line|
  id, length, name, rating = line.chomp.split(/\s*\|\s*/)
  if rating.to_i <= 14
        hours, mins = length.split(/:/)
        min_length = hours.to_i*60+ mins.to_i
        if min_length < 125
                puts "\aYAY! We can watch #{name}"
        else
                puts "Cannot watch #{name}, too long"
        end
  else
        puts "Cannot watch #{name}, only suitable for #{rating}"
  end
end

#=>
Cannot watch Skyfall, too long
Cannot watch The Hurt Locker, only suitable for 15
Cannot watch 21 Jump Street, only suitable for 15
YAY! We can watch Finding Nemo
```

CHAPTER 4

■ ■ ■

Arrays

Ruby arrays are integer-indexed arrays starting at position 0, rather like Java or C. Negative values can be used to retrieve values from the array from the end, so –1 would show the last element of an array, and –2 would show the second from last element.

```
2.1.0 :001 > array = [1,10,3,1]
 => [1, 10, 3, 1]
2.1.0 :002 > array[0]
 => 1
2.1.0 :003 > array[-1]
 => 1
2.1.0 :004 > array[-2]
 => 3
```

Creating Arrays

An array can be created within ruby in a number of different syntaxes, the simplest is the use of the literal constructor []. Arrays are not type dependent, and therefore can contain multiple data types such as another array, a string and an integer.

```
2.1.0 :001 > array = [2, "Hello", 10.02]
 => [2, "Hello", 10.02]
```

An array can also be initialized by using the new method from the Array class; this can be called with 0, 1, or 2 arguments. The first optional parameter is the number of elements to initialize the array with; the second optional parameter is the default value for each of these elements.

```
2.1.0 :001 > array = Array.new
 => []
2.1.0 :002 > Array.new(5)
 => [nil, nil, nil, nil, nil]
2.1.0 :003 > Array.new(4, 10.00)
 => [10.0, 10.0, 10.0, 10.0]
```

Note that the default value is populated into each element of the array, and therefore is only normally used to initialize an array that will be updated afterward.

To set an array to have default elements that are objects, rather than primitive data-types, the block syntax can be used instead:

```
2.1.1 :001 > array = Array.new(4) {Hash.new}
 => [{}, {}, {}, {}]
```

Accessing Array Elements

Within Ruby, a number of methods are made available to us, in order to access array elements, like used previously when accessing strings as shown previously.

The [] method can be used to retrieve individual elements, using the integer index position (starting from 0):

```
2.1.1 :001 > array = [1,10,3,1]
 => [1, 10, 3, 1]
2.1.1 :002 > array[0]
 => 1
2.1.1 :003 > array[3]
 => 1
2.1.1 :004 > array[2]
 => 3
```

Again, similar to accessing a string, a negative index position can be used:

```
2.1.1 :001 > array = [1,10,3,1]
 => [1, 10, 3, 1]
2.1.1 :002 > array[-2]
 => 3
```

Alternatively, pairs and ranges of indexes can be used to extract portions of the array. A pair of indexes is shown as the initial position, followed by the length to extract:

```
2.1.1 :001 > array = [1,10,3,1]
 => [1, 10, 3, 1]
2.1.1 :002 > array[1,3]
 => [10, 3, 1]
2.1.1 :003 > array[1..2]
 => [10, 3]
```

In addition to the preceding methods of extracting data by position, Ruby provides an at method that works identically to the [ ] method

```
2.1.1 :001 > array = [1,10,3,1]
 => [1, 10, 3, 1]
2.1.1 :002 > array.at(1)
 => 10
2.1.1 :003 > array.at(5)
 => nil
```

Using the preceding methods can cause an issue when attempting to extract an element, which does not exist from the array; this would be returned as a nil value. As an alternative we can use the fetch method, which takes a default value on the element not existing within our array.

```
2.1.1 :001 > array = [1,10,3,1]
 => [1, 10, 3, 1]
2.1.1 :002 > array.at(5)
 => nil
2.1.1 :003 > array[5]
 => nil
2.1.1 :004 > array.fetch(5)
IndexError: index 5 outside of array bounds: -4...4
        from (irb):4:in `fetch'
        from (irb):4
        from /Users/matt/.rvm/rubies/ruby-2.1.1/bin/irb:11:in `<main>'
2.1.1 :005 > array.fetch(5,"error")
 => "error"
```

Accessing Array Elements (Part 2)

Similar to the string extraction, we also have a number of methods that can be used with an array to extract data and information about the array. Using the method named "methods" will detail a list of all available methods that we can use to extract data from our array:

```
2.1.1 :001 > [1,2,6].methods
 => [:inspect, :to_s, :to_a, :to_h, :to_ary, :frozen?, :==, :eql?, :hash,
:[], :[]=, :at, :fetch, :first, :last, :concat...
```

A few of these are detailed here.

Length – Output the Array Length (we can also use Size or Count):

```
2.1.1 :001 > [1,2,6].length
 => 3
2.1.1 :002 > [1,2,6].size
 => 3
2.1.1 :003 > [1,2,6].count
 => 3
```

First/Last – Output the First/Last element of the array:

```
2.1.1 :001 > [1,2,6].first
 => 1
2.1.1 :002 > [1,2,6].last
 => 6
```

Sample – Output a random element of the array:

```
2.1.1 :001 > [1,2,6].sample
 => 6
2.1.1 :002 > [1,2,6].sample
 => 1
2.1.1 :003 > [1,2,6].sample
 => 1
```

Empty – Query whether the array is empty:

```
2.1.1 :001 > [1,2,6].empty?
 => false
```

Include – Check whether the array contains an element with a particular value:

```
2.1.1 :001 > [1,2,6].include?(5)
 => false
```

Sort – Reorders the array by values:

```
2.1.1 :001 > [1,6,2].sort
 => [1, 2, 6]
```

Shuffle – Randomizes the order of the arrays elements:

```
2.1.1 :014 > [1,6,2].shuffle
 => [2, 6, 1]
2.1.1 :015 > [1,6,2].shuffle
 => [2, 1, 6]
```

Adding/Removing Items from an Array

Within Ruby we can also add and remove items within an array after the array is initialized. Depending on the action required and the position of the new elements, there are a number of methods available.

Adding a new element to the end of an array:

```
2.1.1 :001 > [1,6,2].push(10)
 => [1, 6, 2, 10]
```

An alternative syntax to push is <<:

```
2.1.1 :003 > [1,6,2] << 10
 => [1, 6, 2, 10]
```

However the push method adds an element to the end of an array; if we need to add an element to the beginning of an array we can instead use unshift:

```
2.1.1 :004 > [1,6,2].unshift(10)
 => [10, 1, 6, 2]
```

If we need to add an element (or elements) to the middle of an array, we can use the insert method. For this we specify the index position (beginning at 0) for the insert, and the elements to insert:

```
2.1.1 :005 > [1,6,2].insert(2,10)
 => [1, 6, 10, 2]
2.1.1 :006 > [1,6,2].insert(2,10,12)
 => [1, 6, 10, 12, 2]
```

The preceding methods allow us to add elements to various positions of an array; we have similar methods available to remove elements from an array. The pop method is the reverse of the push method; simply removing the last element:

```
2.1.1 :001 > array = [1,6,2]
 => [1, 6, 2]
2.1.1 :002 > array.pop
 => 2
2.1.1 :003 > array
 => [1, 6]
```

To retrieve, and remove the first element from the array we use shift (the opposite of unshift):

```
2.1.1 :001 > array = [1,6,2]
 => [1, 6, 2]
2.1.1 :002 > array.shift
 => 1
2.1.1 :003 > array
 => [6, 2]
```

Like the insert method, we can use a delete_at method to delete a specific position of an array:

```
2.1.1 :001 > array = [1,6,2]
 => [1, 6, 2]
2.1.1 :002 > array.delete_at(1)
 => 6
2.1.1 :003 > array
 => [1, 2]
```

We can also use a delete method to delete by value, rather than by position:

```
2.1.1 :001 > array = [1,6,2]
 => [1, 6, 2]
2.1.1 :002 > array.delete(6)
 => 6
2.1.1 :003 > array
 => [1, 2]
```

The previous methods allow us to add and remove specific values to specific positions. If we need to clean up arrays that contain nil or duplicate values, we have two methods available. The first is compact, for removing nil values:

```
2.1.1 :001 > array = [1,6,nil,2,nil]
 => [1, 6, nil, 2, nil]
2.1.1 :002 > array.compact
 => [1, 6, 2]
2.1.1 :003 > array
 => [1, 6, nil, 2, nil]
2.1.1 :004 > array.compact!
 => [1, 6, 2]
2.1.1 :005 > array
 => [1, 6, 2]
```

Notice, that the initial compact method simply strips the nil values and displays them, to update the array object itself, we need to use a compact! method instead.

Likewise we can use a uniq method to remove duplicate values from an array. Note that as per the compact method, we also need to use the uniq! method to update the array variable:

```
2.1.1 :001 > array = [1,6,1,1,nil,2]
 => [1, 6, 1, 1, nil, 2]
2.1.1 :002 > array.uniq
 => [1, 6, nil, 2]
2.1.1 :003 > array
 => [1, 6, 1, 1, nil, 2]
```

```
2.1.1 :004 > array.uniq!
 => [1, 6, nil, 2]
2.1.1 :005 > array
 => [1, 6, nil, 2]
```

Looping Through Arrays

Like all enumerable objects within Ruby, an array has an each method for iterating through the elements within the array.

```
2.1.1 :001 > array = [1,6,1,1,2,1]
 => [1, 6, 1, 1, 2, 1]
2.1.1 :002 > array.each { |item| print item, " " }
1 6 1 1 2 1  => [1, 6, 1, 1, 2, 1]
```

Likewise, if we want to print items in a reverse order we can replace the each method, with a reverse_each method.

```
2.1.1 :001 > array = [1,6,1,1,2,1]
 => [1, 6, 1, 1, 2, 1]
2.1.1 :002 > array.reverse_each { |item| print item, " " }
1 2 1 1 6 1  => [1, 6, 1, 1, 2, 1]
```

With the each method, even if we update the elements value, this does not change the initial array. Instead we can use the map method to output the changed elements, or the map! method to change the original array.

```
2.1.1 :001 > array = [1,6,1,1,2,1]
 => [1, 6, 1, 1, 2, 1]
2.1.1 :002 > array.each { |item| item-1 }
 => [1, 6, 1, 1, 2, 1]
2.1.1 :003 > array.map { |item| item-1 }
 => [0, 5, 0, 0, 1, 0]
2.1.1 :004 > array
 => [1, 6, 1, 1, 2, 1]
2.1.1 :005 > array.map! { |item| item-1 }
 => [0, 5, 0, 0, 1, 0]
2.1.1 :006 > array
 => [0, 5, 0, 0, 1, 0]
```

While these methods are extremely useful for looping through an array, these simply loop through the elements within the array. We can also use a method each_with_index, which pulls through two items with each iteration of the loop, the index and the value

```
2.1.1 :002 > array.each_with_index { |item,index| puts "#{index} = #{item}"
}
0 = Hello
1 = World
2 = Welcome
 => ["Hello", "World", "Welcome"]
```

Selecting Elements from an Array

Using Ruby we have a number of methods to select elements from an array. This works similar to the each or reverse_each method, but allows selective filtering of these arrays to further limit the elements within the array. We have two types of selection methods:

- *Non-destructive methods:* These are simply the limiting of an array without making any changes to the original array once we are finished selecting from it.

- *Destructive methods:* These are methods that limit down an array, but then make changes to the original array.

Starting with the non-destructive methods, we can select (only include this range) and reject/drop_while (exclude this range):

```
2.1.1 :001 > array = [1,2,3,4,5,6,7,8]
 => [1, 2, 3, 4, 5, 6, 7, 8]
2.1.1 :002 > array.select { |item| item > 5 }
 => [6, 7, 8]
2.1.1 :003 > array.reject { |item| item > 5 }
 => [1, 2, 3, 4, 5]
2.1.1 :004 > array.drop_while { |item| item < 5 }
 => [5, 6, 7, 8]
2.1.1 :005 > array
 => [1, 2, 3, 4, 5, 6, 7, 8]
```

Alternatively we could use similar selection methods with destructive methods, which will affect the final array:

```
2.1.1 :001 > array = [1,2,3,4,5,6,7,8]
 => [1, 2, 3, 4, 5, 6, 7, 8]
2.1.1 :002 > array.delete_if { |item| item > 5 }
 => [1, 2, 3, 4, 5]
2.1.1 :003 > array
 => [1, 2, 3, 4, 5]
```

```
2.1.1 :001 > array = [1,2,3,4,5,6,7,8]
 => [1, 2, 3, 4, 5, 6, 7, 8]
2.1.1 :002 > array.keep_if { |item| item > 5 }
 => [6, 7, 8]
2.1.1 :003 > array
 => [6, 7, 8]
```

Exercise

Now we can utilize a number of array methods to replicate the example within Chapter 3.
Rather than using string adaption/extraction we can instead use arrays and array
methods to replicate the same result.

```
dvds = Array.new

dvds.push([100000,[2,17],"Skyfall",12])
dvds.push([100001,[2,06],"The Hurt Locker",15])
dvds.push([100002,[1,45],"21 Jump Street",15])
dvds.push([100003,[1,40],"Finding Nemo",'U'])

dvds.map { |item| item[1] = item[1][0]*60+item[1][1]}

dvds.delete_if { |item| item[3].to_i >=14}

dvds.keep_if { |item| item[1] < 125 }

dvds.each { |item| print "\aYAY! We can watch ", item[2], "\n" }

#=>
YAY! We can watch Finding Nemo
```

CHAPTER 5

■ ■ ■

Hashes

A *hash* in Ruby is a dictionary-style collection, also known as an associative array in other programming languages. Rather than using integer-based indexes, a hash uses any object as the key.

Creating Hashes

To create a hash within Ruby, we can simply use the {} braces, surrounding a set of elements. We can also initialize an empty hash using the empty {} braces:

```
2.1.1 :001 > score = { "Joe Bloggs" => 10, "Sarah Bloggs" => 8 }
 => {"Joe Bloggs"=>10, "Sarah Bloggs"=>8}
2.1.1 :002 > stock = {}
 => {}
```

When creating a hash, an alternative syntax is available using symbols as the index, this is shown by using the :key_name syntax, which can also be written without the initial colons:

```
2.1.1 :001 > stock = { :books => 25, :cds => 7 }
 => {:books=>25, :cds=>7}
2.1.1 :002 > stock = { books: 25, cds: 7 }
 => {:books=>25, :cds=>7}
```

A hash can also be initialized using the new method:

```
2.1.1 :001 > stock = Hash.new
 => {}
2.1.1 :002 > stock[:books] = 25
 => 25
2.1.1 :003 > stock[:cds] = 7
 => 7
2.1.1 :004 > stock  => {:books=>25, :cds=>7}
```

We can also assign a default value to use when attempting to retrieve a key that does not exist within the hash:

```
2.1.1 :001 > stock = Hash.new(0)
 => {}
2.1.1 :002 > stock[:books] = 25
 => 25
2.1.1 :003 > stock[:dvds]
 => 0
```

Alternatively, we can set the default parameter on an existing hash:

```
2.1.1 :001 > stock = { :books => 25, :cds => 7 }
 => {:books=>25, :cds=>7}
2.1.1 :002 > stock.default = 0
 => 0
2.1.1 :003 > stock[:dvds]
 => 0
```

Hash Information

Just like other data types, we have a number of methods available to view meta-data style information about a hash and its elements.

Possibly the simplest method is the ability to show the number of elements within a hash:

```
2.1.1 :001 > score = { "Joe Bloggs" => 10, "Sarah Bloggs" => 8 }
 => {"Joe Bloggs"=>10, "Sarah Bloggs"=>8}
2.1.1 :002 > score.count
 => 2
2.1.1 :003 > score.size
 => 2
2.1.1 :004 > score.length
 => 2
```

To determine whether a hash is empty, we can use the simple empty? method, which returns true or false:

```
2.1.1 :001 > score = { "Joe Bloggs" => 10, "Sarah Bloggs" => 8 }
 => {"Joe Bloggs"=>10, "Sarah Bloggs"=>8}
2.1.1 :002 > score.empty?
 => false
2.1.1 :003 > stock = {}
 => {}
2.1.1 :004 > stock.empty?
 => true
```

We can also determine whether two hashes are identical by using the eql? method:

```
2.1.1 :001 > score = { "Joe Bloggs" => 10, "Sarah Bloggs" => 8 }
 => {"Joe Bloggs"=>10, "Sarah Bloggs"=>8}
2.1.1 :002 > grades = { "Joe Bloggs" => 10, "Sarah Bloggs" => 8 }
 => {"Joe Bloggs"=>10, "Sarah Bloggs"=>8}
2.1.1 :003 > score.eql? grades
 => true
2.1.1 :004 > grades = { "Joe Bloggs" => 10, "Sarah Bloggs" => 9 }
 => {"Joe Bloggs"=>10, "Sarah Bloggs"=>9}
2.1.1 :005 > score.eql? grades
 => false
```

If we need to expose whether the hash contains a particular key or value, we can utilize the has_key? and has_value? methods:

```
2.1.1 :001 > score = { "Joe Bloggs" => 10, "Sarah Bloggs" => 8 }
 => {"Joe Bloggs"=>10, "Sarah Bloggs"=>8}
2.1.1 :002 > score.has_key? "Joe Bloggs"
 => true
2.1.1 :003 > score.has_key? "John Bloggs"
 => false
2.1.1 :004 > score.has_value? 3
 => false
2.1.1 :005 > score.has_value? 8
 => true
```

Sorting Hash Elements

To complete basic sorting on a hash within Ruby, we can utilize the sort method:

```
2.1.1 :001 > stock = { 25 => "Books", 7 => "CDs", 2 => "DVDs" }
 => {25=>"Books", 7=>"CDs", 2=>"DVDs"}
2.1.1 :002 > stock.sort
 => [[2, "DVDs"], [7, "CDs"], [25, "Books"]]
```

Accessing Hash Elements

To retrieve hash elements, rather like an array, you address the hash symbol with the hash [key] syntax:

```
2.1.1 :001 > stock = { :books => 25, :cds => 7 }
 => {:books=>25, :cds=>7}
2.1.1 :002 > stock[:books]
 => 25
```

We can also utilize other types of keys, such as the strings used previously in the first example:

```
2.1.1 :001 > score = { "Joe Bloggs" => 10, "Sarah Bloggs" => 8 }
 => {"Joe Bloggs"=>10, "Sarah Bloggs"=>8}
2.1.1 :002 > score["Joe Bloggs"]
 => 10
```

Hashes are commonly used when passing named parameters into a method, where the number and order of parameters can differ depending on what is required. With using a traditional set of parameters, nil or empty data would have to be passed during the method call, and filtered out later; instead a hash can be used. If a hash is used as the last parameter to a method, no braces are required either.

```
class Score
def self.register(params)
        @name = params[:name]
        @score  = params[:score]
        puts "#{@name} got a score of #{@score}"
end
end

Score.register(name: "Joe Bloggs", score: 10)
 => Joe Bloggs got a score of 10
```

We can also utilize a select method to pass a statement to the hash, in order to select a range of elements:

```
2.1.1 :001 > stock = { :books => 25, :cds => 7, :dvds => 2 }
 => {:books=>25, :cds=>7, :dvds=>2}
2.1.1 :002 > stock.select{|type,quantity| quantity > 5 }
 => {:books=>25, :cds=>7}
```

Looping Through Hashes

At times, we need to loop through hashes rather than retrieving individual elements, to do this utilize the each method.

```
scores = {
        "John" => 10,
        "Paul" => 8,
        "Sarah" => 9
}
scores.each do|name,score|
   puts "#{name}: #{score}"
end
```

This outputs:

```
John: 10
Paul: 8
Sarah: 9
```

Hashes are unordered unlike arrays, and therefore will not necessarily be looped through in the order that elements are inserted.

To shortcut the syntax for this, we can use each_value and each_key instead if only the keys or values are required:

```
scores = { "John" => 10, "Paul" => 8, "Sarah" => 9 }
scores.each_key do|name|
  puts "#{name}"
end

=>
John
Paul
Sarah

scores = { "John" => 10, "Paul" => 8, "Sarah" => 9 }
scores.each_value do|score|
  puts "#{score}"
end

=>
10
8
9
```

Altering Hashes

Rather like an array, we have a number of methods available in order to alter and manipulate hashes, such as deleting elements by the key:

```
2.1.1 :001 > stock = {:books => 2, :cds => 7}
 => {:books=>2, :cds=>7}
2.1.1 :002 > stock.delete(:books)
 => 2
2.1.1 :003 > stock
 => {:cds=>7}
```

Likewise, under certain scenarios we can utilize a delete_if method if we need to delete elements within a hash based upon the value (or the key):

```
2.1.1 :001 > stock = {:books => 2, :cds => 7, :dvds => 200}
 => {:books=>2, :cds=>7, :dvds=>200}
2.1.1 :002 > stock.delete_if {|key, value| value < 3 }
 => {:cds=>7, :dvds=>200}
2.1.1 :003 > stock.delete_if {|key, value| key == :dvds }
 => {:cds=>7}
```

We can reverse this logic and use a keep_if instead, where all matching elements from the block are kept and any which return false are deleted:

```
2.1.1 :001 > stock = {:books => 2, :cds => 7, :dvds => 200}
 => {:books=>2, :cds=>7, :dvds=>200}
2.1.1 :002 > stock.keep_if {|key, value| value < 3 }
 => {:books=>2}
```

We can also clear a hash of all elements if required:

```
2.1.1 :001 > stock = {:books => 2, :cds => 7, :dvds => 200}
 => {:books=>2, :cds=>7, :dvds=>200}
2.1.1 :002 > stock.clear
 => {}
```

Similar to an array, we can use a shift method to remove an element from the hash. However, note that as a hash's order is not guaranteed, there is no control over which key/value pair is being deleted. This is, however, useful during a loop.

```
stock = {:books => 2, :cds => 7, :dvds => 200}
until stock.empty?
        name, stock_level = stock.shift
        puts "Removing stock for #{name}: #{stock_level}"
end

Removing stock for books: 2
Removing stock for cds: 7
Removing stock for dvds: 200
```

Merging Hashes

There are times when you will have two hashes (such as an internal variable and a set of parameters passed in to a method), which you need to merge to have one hash to iterate through. Ruby has a merge method for a hash, which can merge two hashes. If you are merging a hash with the same keys, the new hash being merged in will win on any conflicts unless otherwise specified:

```
stock1 = {:books => 2, :cds => 7}
stock2 = {:cds => 2, :dvds => 7}
stock1.merge(stock2)
 => {:books=>2, :cds=>2, :dvds=>7}
stock1
 => {:books=>2, :cds=>7}
stock1.merge!(stock2)
 => {:books=>2, :cds=>2, :dvds=>7}
stock1
 => {:books=>2, :cds=>2, :dvds=>7}
```

Note that we have to use the merge! method instead if we want the stock1 hash updated, rather than just the result of the merge returned.

```
stock1 = {:books => 2, :cds => 7}
stock2 = {:cds => 2, :dvds => 7}
stock1.merge(stock2){|key, oldvalue, newvalue| newvalue+oldvalue}
 => {:books=>2, :cds=>9, :dvds=>7}
```

As you can see from the preceding code, we have used a block for matching keys to have their values added together, rather than just the new hash winning conflicts.

Exercise

As in previous chapters, we can now utilize a number of methods linked to hashes to complete an example.

```
dvds = Hash.new

dvds["Skyfall"] = {:id => 100000, :hours => 2, :mins => 17, :classification
=> 12}
dvds["The Hurt Locker"] = {:id => 100001, :hours => 2, :mins => 6,
:classification => 15}
dvds["21 Jump Street"] = {:id => 100002, :hours => 1, :mins => 45,
:classification => 15}
dvds["Finding Nemo"] = {:id => 100003, :hours => 1, :mins => 40,
:classification => 'U'}
```

```
dvds.each do|name,details|
details[:mins] = details[:mins] + (details[:hours]*60)
end

dvds.delete_if { |name,details| details[:classification].to_i >=14}

dvds.keep_if { |name,details| details[:mins] < 125 }

dvds.each_key { |name| print "\aYAY! We can watch ", name, "\n" }
```

■ ■ ■

## CHAPTER 6

Numbers

The Numeric class within Ruby is a containing class for the Integer and Float classes. This contains all methods linked to numeric variables either with (float) or without (integer) decimal places. The Numeric class is a very simple class, which holds the ability to perform a number of complex calculations with numbers.

Creating Numbers

Creating a number in Ruby is extremely simple, rather like creating a String. Rather than using a New method, or a set of braces, like an array or hash, a Number is created by setting a variable without quotation marks. If the number contains a decimal place, it is created as a float; if the number is without a decimal place, it is created as an integer

```
2.1.1 :001 > number = 10
 => 10
2.1.1 :002 > number.is_a?(Integer)
 => true
2.1.1 :003 > number = 10.2
 => 10.2
2.1.1 :004 > number.is_a?(Integer)
 => false
2.1.1 :005 > number.is_a?(Float)
 => true
```

This is one of the reasons that Ruby's loosely typed structure is a very powerful tool.

Numeric Alterations

As with most data types within Ruby, we will need to make some alterations to variables stored. A number is one of the most manipulated data types within Ruby, due to its uses in mathematical calculations, and loop counting. Within Ruby there are a number of methods, and additional ways of manipulating numbers, the simplest being mathematical symbols.

```
2.1.1 :001 > number = 10
 => 10
2.1.1 :002 > number = number + 2
 => 12
2.1.1 :003 > number = number - 5
 => 7
2.1.1 :004 > number = number * 2
 => 14
2.1.1 :005 > number = number / 7
 => 2
```

Ruby will not always adjust the data type between an Integer and Float as required. Note that Ruby classes an Integer as a Fixnum, and a Float as a Float

```
2.1.1 :001 > number = 10
 => 10
2.1.1 :002 > number.class
 => Fixnum
2.1.1 :003 > number = number + 2
 => 12
2.1.1 :004 > number.class
 => Fixnum
2.1.1 :005 > number / 4
 => 2 #Notice this should be 2.5
2.1.1 :006 > number.class
 => Fixnum
2.1.1 :007 > number = 10
 => 10
2.1.1 :008 > number.class
 => Fixnum
2.1.1 :009 > number = number / 6.5
 => 1.5384615384615385 #Notice a conversion has taken place as the divider
    was a float
2.1.1 :010 > number.class
 => Float
```

In addition to simple mathematical arithmetic, we have the ability to call methods in order to return various calculations of a number. The first, is the + or – of the initial number. This will return the unary positive or negative of the number (i.e. the original number, or the negative of the number

```
2.1.1 :001 > number = 10
 => 10
2.1.1 :002 > +number
 => 10
2.1.1 :003 > -number
 => -10
```

```
2.1.1 :004 > number = -5
 => -5
2.1.1 :005 > +number
 => -5
2.1.1 :006 > -number
 => 5
```

In addition, we may be required to find out the absolute value of the number, this is, the positive value of the number, regardless as to whether the original number is positive, or negative.

```
2.1.1 :001 > number = 10
 => 10
2.1.1 :002 > number.abs
 => 10
2.1.1 :003 > number = -4
 => -4
2.1.1 :004 > number.abs
 => 4
```

If we have a float value, and wish to round this to the next or previous decimal number, we can use the ceil or floor methods. The ceil (for ceiling) method rounds the number to the next decimal number. The floor method rounds the number to the previous decimal number

```
2.1.1 :001 > number = 11.5
 => 11.5
2.1.1 :002 > number.ceil
 => 12
2.1.1 :003 > number.floor
 => 11
2.1.1 :004 > number = 3.1
 => 3.1
2.1.1 :005 > number.ceil
 => 4
2.1.1 :006 > number.floor
 => 3
```

We also have the ability to perform a natural, mathematical round in order to round the number up or down as expected. A .4 will round down, a .6 will round up, and ties will round up, so a .5 will also round up

```
2.1.1 :001 > number = 10.6
 => 10.6
2.1.1 :002 > number.round
 => 11
```

```
2.1.1 :003 > number = 10.4
 => 10.4
2.1.1 :004 > number.round
 => 10
2.1.1 :005 > number = 10.5
 => 10.5
2.1.1 :006 > number.round
 => 11
```

In addition to the / divide operator, we have a div method in order to perform a division to a number

```
2.1.1 :001 > number = 10
 => 10
2.1.1 :002 > number = number.div 5
 => 2
```

Whilst this is useful, we discovered that conversions do not always change the data type, therefore dividing 10 by 4 should output 2.5; however as the data type is an Integer this will actually output 2. We can therefore use remainder method to find out the remainder of the division.

```
2.1.1 :001 > number = 10
 => 10
2.1.1 :002 > number = number.remainder 4
 => 2
```

We could, instead, use the modulo method instead of the remainder method. The modulo outputs the remainder again; however the remainder method rounds the calculated value towards 0, where as the modulo rounds downwards. The remainder also always outputs the same sign (positive/negative) as the original number.

```
2.1.1 :001 > number = 10
 => 10
2.1.1 :002 > number = number.modulo 4
 => 2
2.1.1 :003 > number = -10
 => -10
2.1.1 :004 > number.modulo 4
 => 2
2.1.1 :005 > number.remainder 4
 => -2
```

Whilst these are all useful, they require multiple calculations to run a division, and then calculate the remainder. Instead we can use the divmod method to return an array of the division, then the modulo methods calculation.

```
2.1.1 :001 > number = 10
 => 10
2.1.1 :002 > number.divmod 4
 => [2, 2]
2.1.1 :003 > number = -10
 => -10
2.1.1 :004 > number.divmod 4
 => [-3, 2]
```

The main issue we have seen previously is the lack of automatically converting the Numeric Type when a division leaves a remainder. There are times that we require an exact calculation, rather than just a remainder. For this Ruby has a quo method, which divides (as per the div method) and returns a float when dividing floats, or rational's for all other scenarios. *Note that rational's can be cast to floats*

```
2.1.1 :001 > number = 10
 => 10
2.1.1 :002 > number.quo 2
 => (5/1)
2.1.1 :003 > number = 10
 => 10
2.1.1 :004 > number = number.quo 4
 => (5/2)
2.1.1 :005 > number.to_f
 => 2.5
```

Numeric Comparisons

Previously we have used a number of mathematical formulae, and methods in order to alter the value or Numeric variables, however at times we need to compare numbers in order to calculate whether they meet a certain criteria. Again we can utilize a number of mathematical comparators, and methods.

The first sets of mathematical comparators are the greater than, greater than/equals to, less than, less than/equals to

```
2.1.1 :001 > number = 10
 => 10
2.1.1 :002 > number > 5
 => true
2.1.1 :003 > number >= 10
 => true
2.1.1 :004 > number < 5
 => false
2.1.1 :005 > number <= 10
 => true
```

We can also utilize the == comparator to check for equal values

```
2.1.1 :001 > 10 == 10
 => true
2.1.1 :002 > 10 == 10.0
 => true
2.1.1 :003 > 10 == 11
 => false
2.1.1 :004 > 10 == 10.001
 => false
```

The final comparator we can utilize is the "spaceship" operator. This returns -1 if the original is less than the comparison, 0 if they are equal, and +1 if the original is greater than the comparison. This comparator is used to calculate the previous such as greater than and less than.

```
2.1.1 :001 > 10 <=> 11
 => -1
2.1.1 :002 > 10 <=> 9
 => 1
2.1.1 :003 > 10 <=> 10
 => 0
```

We can also utilize other methods in order to compare Numeric values. The simplest of these is the eql? method, which simply returns the same output as the == operator. Note however that the == operator will often cast an integer with an added decimal place (such as 10.0) whereas the eql? method will not cast.

```
2.1.1 :001 > 10.eql? 10
 => true
2.1.1 :002 > 10.eql? 10.0
 => false
2.1.1 :003 > 10.eql? 11
 => false
2.1.1 :004 > 10.eql? 10.001
 => false
```

In order to check types, we have the integer? method to check whether the number passed in is an integer type, again note that no casting takes place

```
2.1.1 :001 > 10.integer?
 => true
2.1.1 :002 > 10.2.integer?
 => false
2.1.1 :003 > 10.0.integer?
 => false
2.1.1 :004 > -1.integer?
 => true
```

We can check whether the Numeric value is equals (or not equals) to zero. Notice here that the zero method returns true or false booleans, whereas the nonzero method returns the non-zero value (or a nil if the value is 0)

```
2.1.1 :001 > 10.zero?
 => false
2.1.1 :002 > 0.zero?
 => true
2.1.1 :003 > 10.nonzero?
 => 10
2.1.1 :004 > 0.nonzero?
 => nil
```

In order to find out whether a value is odd or even, we can use the odd? and even? methods.

```
2.1.1 :001 > 10.odd?
 => false
2.1.1 :002 > 10.even?
 => true
2.1.1 :003 > 15.odd?
 => true
2.1.1 :004 > 15.even?
 => false
2.1.1 :005 > 0.even?
 => true
2.1.1 :006 > 0.odd?
 => false
```

In addition to the mathematical comparators we used previously, we have the ability to check whether a particular Numeric value or variable is between an allowed range. For this we use the between? method, which accepts 2 parameters as the 2 bound values.

```
2.1.1 :001 > 10.between?(5,15)
 => true
2.1.1 :002 > 15.between?(5,15)
 => true
2.1.1 :003 > 16.between?(5,15)
 => false
2.1.1 :004 > 5.between?(5,5)
 => true
2.1.1 :005 > 6.between?(5,5)
 => false
```

In order to easily increment in steps, we can use the upto method, which accepts a single parameter, followed by a block to be run for each iteration of the loop.

```
2.1.1 :001 > 10.upto(16) { |i| puts i }
10
11
12
13
14
15
16
 => 10
2.1.1 :002 > -5.upto(-10) { |i| puts i }
 => -5
2.1.1 :003 > -10.upto(-5) { |i| puts i }
-10
-9
-8
-7
-6
-5
 => -10
```

Exercise

As previously, we can utilize a number of Numeric methods in order to further advance our DVD selector application. Notice that we have advanced our Array example, and set the length in minutes in order to utilize the quo method in order to calculate all films that are under 2 hours in length. We are also checking that the age bracket of our movies is between 10 and 15.

```
dvds = Array.new

dvds.push([100000,137,"Skyfall",12])
dvds.push([100001,114,"The Hurt Locker",15])
dvds.push([100002,105,"21 Jump Street",15])
dvds.push([100003,100,"Finding Nemo",'U'])

dvds.delete_if { |item| item[3].to_i.between?(10,15)}

dvds.keep_if { |item| item[1].quo(60).to_f < 2 }

dvds.each { |item| print "\aYAY! We can watch ", item[2], "\n" }

#=>
YAY! We can watch Finding Nemo
```

CHAPTER 7

■ ■ ■

Booleans

Booleans within Ruby are actually known as parts of the TrueClass and FalseClass, rather than a Boolean Data Type as such. It is worth noting that nil (Ruby's version of a null) is not a Boolean.

```
2.1.1 :001 > true.class
 => TrueClass
2.1.1 :002 > false.class
 => FalseClass
```

Creating Boolean Values

Creating a Boolean value within Ruby is similar to creating a String/Numeric value. You simply set a variable to the value required (true or false):

```
2.1.1 :001 > test = true
 => true
2.1.1 :002 > puts test
true
 => nil
2.1.1 :003 > test.class
 => TrueClass
```

Expression Tests

Within Ruby a number of expression tests return a Boolean value; which is most often used when writing an if/else if/else statement. Ruby tests the conditions and returns a true or false to determine the code to be executed:

```
2.1.1 :001 > age = 24
 => 24
2.1.1 :002 > age >=20
 => true
```

Ruby can also utilize the and/or operators to evaluate multiple conditions:

```
2.1.1 :001 > age = 24
 => 24
2.1.1 :002 > name = "Joe"
 => "Joe"
2.1.1 :003 > age >=20 && name == "Paul"
 => false
2.1.1 :004 > age >=20 || name == "Paul"
 => true
```

Ruby also negates expressions by using the ! operator (meaning not):

```
2.1.1 :001 > age = 24
 => 24
2.1.1 :002 > ! ( age >=20 )
 => false
2.1.1 :003 > ! ( age < 20 )
 => true
```

While this shorthand conditional logic is useful for simple checks, when we need to test multiple conditions, possibly nest other conditional logic within these, we can use alternative syntax; such as the standard if/else if/else syntax. It is worth noting that the if brackets in the code that follows are optional within Ruby, unlike other programming languages.

```
#!/usr/bin/env ruby

age = 24
name = "Joe"

if ( age > 20 )
        if( name == "Paul" )
                puts "Hello Paul"
        elsif( name == "Joe" )
                puts "Hello Joe"
        else
                puts "Hello somebody?"
        end
else
        puts "Sorry, you're not old enough to enter"
end

#=> Hello Joe
```

For the simpler statements, we can use a shorthand:

```
( condition ? value if true : value if false )
```

Such as:

```
2.1.1 :001 > age = 24
 => 24
2.1.1 :002 > ( age > 20 ? "Yes" : "No" )
 => "Yes"
```

Within Ruby we have Double Bang, also known as a Bang-Bang, that takes a value and casts it directly to a Boolean. It is worth noting however that only a nil returns false; all others return true.

```
2.1.1 :001 > !!0
 => true
2.1.1 :002 > !!1
 => true
2.1.1 :003 > !!nil
 => false
2.1.1 :004 > !!false
 => false
2.1.1 :005 > !!true
 => true
```

Although this does not instantly seem particularly useful, we can use this to determine whether a value is a Boolean.

```
2.1.1 :001 > age = 24
 => 24
2.1.1 :002 > !!age == age
 => false
2.1.1 :003 > test = true
 => true
2.1.1 :004 > !!test == test
 => true
2.1.1 :005 > test_false = false
 => false
2.1.1 :006 > !!test_false == test_false
 => true
```

What happens here is age is casted to a Boolean and then checked against its original value for equality. Whereas 24 as a Boolean is true, this does not match its original value. When we cast true or false to a Boolean they remain as true or false when comparing to their original values.

Comparative Operators

Within Ruby we can use comparative operators to compare the two values on either side of the operator to determine a true or false outcome:

```
2.1.1 :001 > 10 == 10 #Equals
 => true
2.1.1 :002 > 10 != 10 #Not Equals
 => false
2.1.1 :003 > 10 <= 10 #Less than or equals
 => true
2.1.1 :004 > 10 >=10 #Greater than or equals
 => true
2.1.1 :005 > 10 < 10 #Less than
 => false
2.1.1 :006 > 10 > 10 #Greater than
 => false
```

Due to Ruby's loosely typed language, there are a couple of pitfalls when using Booleans. The main one is the loose casting of non-Boolean values to Booleans:

```
#!/usr/bin/env ruby

destroy_forcefully = false

if ( destroy_forcefully )
        puts "Destroying now!"
else
        puts "Are you sure?"
end

#=> Are you sure?
```

This is as we would expect; however if a numeric value of 0 passed over, the user may assume that this would equate to false. This will be casted directly and equate to true.

```
#!/usr/bin/env ruby

destroy_forcefully = 0

puts !!destroy_forcefully.class

if ( destroy_forcefully )
        puts "Destroying now!"
else
```

```
        puts "Are you sure?"
end
#=>
true
Destroying now!
```

Notice we added some debugging to calculate the class type when casting the 0 to a Boolean, this shows that Ruby will cast a 0 to true, rather than the expected false.

CHAPTER 8

■ ■ ■

Objects

In the previous chapters we discussed individual data types within the Ruby programming language and how these all work individually. The final data type we will look at is the Object data type. The Object data type (also known as BasicObject) mixes with the Kernel module to import a number of useful methods, which can be utilized for variousscenarios within Ruby programming.

```
2.1.1 :001 > self.class
 => Object
```

Objects are also associated to Object-Oriented Programming. Object orientation is an alternative to the procedural method of programming. Procedural code runs from top to bottom in a very simple and linear way. Object-Oriented programming includes creating a set of classes, with associated methods (such as a class called Car, with a method called startEngine). We then initialize these classes by creating instance objects of the class to call the method. In this chapter we will focus on the objects themselves and their behavior, rather than the classes at this stage.

```ruby
#!/usr/bin/env ruby

class Car
  def startEngine
    puts "Engine Started"
  end
end

my_car = Car.new
my_car.startEngine

#=>
Engine Started
```

Constants

Within Ruby objects, we have access to a number of constants (meaning that the values never change within the program itself). These constants can be used to read various properties of the running application, configuration, the Ruby run-time being used, and even the outside operating system. These constants include ARGF, ARGV, DATA, ENV, RUBY_*, STDERR, STDIN, STDOUT, TOPLEVEL_BINDING, and TRUE/FALSE/NIL.

ARGF

ARGF is a stream built when passing in a list of files to be processed using arguments to an application, or by using STDIN. As a file is processed by ARGF it is removed from the ARGV array so that it is not re-processed.

test.txt:
```
Test File 1
```

test2.txt:
```
Test File 2
```

fig02.rb:
```ruby
#!/usr/bin/env ruby
puts ARGV.to_s

puts ARGF.readlines

puts ARGV.to_s

#=>
ruby fig02.rb test.txt test2.txt
["test.txt", "test2.txt"]
Test File 1
Test File 2
[]
```

Notice that the Ruby code cast the ARGV array into a string so that we could see the contents; then we used the ARGF constant to parse the values, and a readlines method to read the contents of the two files, followed by re-outputting the ARGV constant to show that it is now empty.

ARGV

The abilities of the ARGV constant have already been demonstrated in the preceding example; however this constant is also useful for passing in values other than just filenames to be processed by using the ARGF constant:

```
#!/usr/bin/env ruby
puts ARGV[0] + ARGV[1]

#=>
ruby fig03.rb 10 5 .........
15
```

We can also use this to have arguments passed in, rather like a normal command line binary application:

```
#!/usr/bin/env ruby
puts ARGV.to_s

#=>
ruby fig04.rb --verbose -f
```

DATA

The DATA constant can be used to read a "data section" of the file to be executed. A data section begins with the __END__ code on a new line, and ends at the end of a file:

```
#!/usr/bin/env ruby
puts DATA.gets
__END__
Hello World!

#=>
ruby fig05.rb
Hello World!
```

ENV

The ENV constant is probably one of the most used constants within Ruby, especially in Ruby on Rails programming. ENV stands for Environment, and it is often used to read various Environmental Variables within Ruby. Note that the output from the inspect method has been trimmed down, as it contains a lot of information within this hash:

```
#!/usr/bin/env ruby
puts ENV['HOME']
```

```
puts ENV.inspect

#=>
ruby fig06.rb

/Users/matt
{ ... "SHELL"=>"/bin/zsh", "HOME"=>"/Users/matt", "USER"=>"matt",
"LOGNAME"=>"matt" ... }
```

RUBY_*

There are a number of RUBY_ based constants that hold useful information about Ruby and its environment as shown in the table that follows.

Ruby Constant	Output	Details
RUBY_COPYRIGHT	ruby - Copyright (C) 1993-2014 Yukihiro Matsumoto	Ruby copyright information
RUBY_DESCRIPTION	ruby 2.1.1p76 (2014-02-24 revision 45161) [x86_64-darwin12.0]	Full Ruby version like ruby –v outputs
RUBY_ENGINE	ruby	The Ruby Engine being used (ruby, or jruby if JRuby is being used)
RUBY_PATCHLEVEL	76	The Ruby Patchset Level (will be -1 for development builds)
RUBY_PLATFORM	x86_64-darwin12.0	Platform on which Ruby is running
RUBY_RELEASE_DATE	2014-02-24	Date on which the current version of Ruby was released
RUBY_REVISION	45161	The Subversion Revision for the current Ruby version
RUBY_VERSION	2.1.1	Short version of the Ruby version running

STDERR

Ruby's Standard Error Output, this is normally mapped to the running console, however can be remapped to a log file to keep track of errors (rather than standard output) separately.

STDIN

The Standard Input, including the input passed in to a script and any input received during the running of the application.

STDOUT

The Standard Output, which is used by default to output any data to the console during the running of an application (such as the output from a puts statement).

TOPLEVEL_BINDING

This is the global instance of Binding that is mapped to the object for the main method when running Ruby.

TRUE/FALSE/NIL

The TRUE, FALSE, and NIL constants are aliases for true, false, and nil used previously within Chapter 7.

Comparisons

As with other data types we have looked at previously, we can use comparisons to compare values of Data Types. Likewise, we can actually compare two instances of an object to check for equality.

```
#!/usr/bin/env ruby

object = "ABC"
new_object = object.dup #Duplicate the object

puts object == new_object
puts object.equal? new_object
puts object.equal? object

#=>
true
false
true
```

It is worth noting that the == equality check between the two objects returned true, as the two objects are identical; however the equal? check requires the two objects to have the same hash key (i.e., point to the same object). Again note that 1 == 1.0 returns true, as they are seen as equal; however the eql? check returns false, as they have different hash keys (one is an integer, the other is a float).

```
#!/usr/bin/env ruby

puts 1 == 1.0
puts 1.eql? 1.0

puts 1.eql? 1

#=>
true
false
true
```

We can also check whether values are set to nil, by using the nil? method:

```
2.1.1 :001 > nil.nil?
 => true
2.1.1 :002 > false.nil?
 => false
2.1.1 :003 > 0.nil?
 => false
```

Duplication of Objects

Within Ruby we can also manipulate objects to clone or duplicate an object.

```
#!/usr/bin/env ruby

class Car
  colour = ""
  def startEngine
    puts "Engine Started"
  end

  def setColour color
    self.colour = colour
        end
end

my_car = Car.new
puts my_car.class

new_car = my_car.clone
puts new_car.class

#=>
Car
Car
```

```ruby
#!/usr/bin/env ruby

class Car
        def startEngine
                puts "Engine Started"
        end
end

my_car = Car.new
puts my_car.class

new_car = my_car.dup
puts new_car.class

#=>
Car
Car
```

While the Duplicate (dup) and Clone methods seem to do the same thing, there are some subtle differences, which need to be taken into consideration. Clone duplicates an object, including its internal state; however Duplicate uses the class that the object is an instance of to create a new instance.

Freezing of Objects

There are times when we need to make an object frozen, or read-only. We want to prevent further modification to the object. On trying to modify a frozen object a RuntimeError is generated:

```ruby
#!/usr/bin/env ruby

results = [ 98, 76, 28 ]

results.freeze
puts results.frozen?

results.pop(10)

#=>
true
fig11.rb:8:in 'pop': can't modify frozen Array (RuntimeError)
        from fig11.rb:8:in '<main>'
```

Object Metadata

As with other data types within Ruby, we can easily determine some metadata regarding an object, such as the Class that it is part of, details about the object, or the methods available.

```ruby
#!/usr/bin/env ruby

class Car
        def startEngine
                puts "Engine Started"
        end
end

my_car = Car.new
puts my_car.class #=> Car
puts my_car.instance_of? Car #=> true
puts my_car.is_a? Car #=> true
```

We can determine the available methods within a class. The methods method shows all public or protected methods:

```ruby
#!/usr/bin/env ruby

class Car
        def startEngine
                puts "Engine Started"
        end
end

my_car = Car.new
puts my_car.methods

#=>

startEngine
nil?
===
=~
!~
eql?
hash
<=> #List continued, but trimmed
```

Alternatively, we use methods such as public_methods, protected_methods, and private_methods to output a list of methods by access types:

```ruby
#!/usr/bin/env ruby

class Car
        def startEngine
                puts "Engine Started"
        end
end

my_car = Car.new

puts "Public Methods"
puts my_car.public_methods
puts "======================="
puts ""

puts "Protected Methods"
puts my_car.protected_methods
puts "======================="
puts ""

puts "Private Methods"
puts my_car.private_methods
puts "======================="
puts ""

#=>
Public Methods
startEngine
nil?
===
=~
!~
eql?
... trimmed ...
=======================

Protected Methods
=======================

Private Methods
initialize_copy
initialize_dup
initialize_clone
sprintf
... trimmed ...
```

Within Ruby we also can inspect an object to return the hash pointer of the object:

```
#!/usr/bin/env ruby

class Car
        def startEngine
                puts "Engine Started"
        end
end

my_car = Car.new
my_car.inspect

#=>
#<Car:0x00000103015e60>
```

CHAPTER 9

■ ■ ■

Loops and Iterators

Previously, we have discussed various data types within Ruby, how these operate, and the methods that we have available. We have also looked at some examples as to using them within an application. We are now going to investigate loops and iterators within Ruby. There are many types of loops/iterators within Ruby, from simple to complex methods.

Loop Method

The simplest type of iterator within Ruby is a loop method. While the name sounds like this is a loop, this is in fact an iterator method. First, we will set up the simplest type of loop, the infinite loop, printing out Hello World on a new line forever.

```
#!/usr/bin/env ruby
loop do
        puts "Hello World"
end

#=>
Hello World
Hello World
Hello World
Hello World
...
```

However, this type of loop is not very useful, as this would continue running forever. Instead we could use a break, next, or redo keyword to alter the running of the loop. First we will use the break keyword, which allows us to exit the loop. We will set i to 0 initially, and then add 1 each time we loop. When i reaches 5, we will break out of the loop:

```
#!/usr/bin/env ruby
i = 0
loop do
        i+=1
        puts "Hello World"
        break if i==5
end
```

```
#=>
Hello World
Hello World
Hello World
Hello World
Hello World
```

We can use the next keyword to skip over the current iteration of the loop, if required:

```
#!/usr/bin/env ruby
i = 0
loop do
        i+=1
        next if i==2
        puts i
        break if i==5
end

#=>
1
3
4
5
```

Using the break keyword, we can get the loop to return a value back to the calling method:

```
#!/usr/bin/env ruby
i = 0
puts(loop do
        i+=1
        puts i
        break 'Hello World' if i==5
end)

#=>
1
2
3
4
5
Hello World
```

Details for the redo keyword appear later, as it doesn't make sense to use it during a loop statement.

While Loop

The while loop is similar to most other programming languages, and works in a similar way to the loop shown previously, with minor changes to the syntax (namely, you specify the break when calling the while loop):

```
#!/usr/bin/env ruby
i = 0
while i < 5
        i+=1
        puts i
end

#=>
1
2
3
4
5
```

Until Loop

The until loop is similar to the while loop, just with the logic inversed:

```
#!/usr/bin/env ruby
i = 0
until i >=5
        i+=1
        puts i
end

#=>
1
2
3
4
5
```

The until loop is the perfect loop to include the redo loop, due to the logic of the until loop:

```
#!/usr/bin/env ruby
i = 0
until i >=2
        i+=1
```

```
        puts i
        redo if i >=2
end

#=>
1
2
3
4
5
6
...
```

The until loop, loops up to the second iteration, but during the last iteration the redo clause is met, and the loop continues. We could instead replace the redo to just redo when the value is 2:

```
#!/usr/bin/env ruby
i = 0
until i >=2
        i+=1
        puts i
        redo if i == 2
end

#=>
1
2
3
```

While and Until Loops – Alternative Syntax

We can also use an alternative syntax when creating while and until loops, which are often ideal for simple loops, and easier to read.

```
#!/usr/bin/env ruby
i = 0
print "#{i+=1} " while i < 5

puts ""

i = 0
print "#{i+=1} " until i == 5

#=>
1 2 3 4 5
1 2 3 4 5
```

We can also use this alternative syntax to create an alternative to the do..while loop, which Ruby doesn't have directly like other programming languages.

```ruby
#!/usr/bin/env ruby
i = 0

begin
        puts i
        i+=1
end while i < 5

#=>
0
1
2
3
4
```

The reason for the do..while loop being so well used within programming languages is due to its constructor always being called at least once, even if the conditions are not met. You will notice in the next example the variable i is already set to 10, and therefore when checking that i must be less than 5, this check fails, and a standard while loop would not run the loop at all. Instead, with a do..while style loop, the loop will be once initially regardless, before the while checks whether the loop should continue running.

```ruby
#!/usr/bin/env ruby
i = 10

begin
        puts i
        i+=1
end while i < 5

#=>
10
```

Likewise, we could replace a while loop used in this way for an until loop:

```ruby
#!/usr/bin/env ruby
i = 10

begin
        puts i
        i+=1
end until i == 11

#=>
10
```

For Loop

The for loop is a span between a loop, and an iterator within Ruby. Although it is officially a loop construct, it acts very similar to an iterator, just without accepting a block. For loops are particularly useful when looping through a range, array, or hash.

```ruby
#!/usr/bin/env ruby
for i in 1..5
 puts i
end

#=>
1
2
3
4
5
```

Or we could use an array instead:

```ruby
#!/usr/bin/env ruby
for val in [1,5,8,10,15]
    puts val
end

#=>
1
5
8
10
15
```

Each Iterator

Now that we have detailed traditional loops, what they offer us, and how we can decide on the most suitable loop to use, we will look at iterators within Ruby. Iterators execute a block (a *block* is simply a section of code that the values are run against) and will iterate in a similar way that a loop was detailed earlier in the chapter. We will start with the each iterator, which is the most simple iterator within Ruby, and works similar to the way that the for loop works.

```ruby
#!/usr/bin/env ruby
vars = [1,5,8,10,15]

vars.each { |value| puts value }
```

```
#=>
1
5
8
10
15
```

The Times Iterator

The times iterator works similar to the way that the for loop works in other programming languages. This runs a block of code *X* number of times.

```
#!/usr/bin/env ruby
5.times { |i| puts i }

#=>
0
1
2
3
4
```

Upto and Step Iterators

The upto and step iterators are again similar to other programming languages for loop, in the sense that rather than a "run this block of code *X* times" statement, you may specify, "run this block of code until i reaches 10".

```
#!/usr/bin/env ruby
1.upto(5) { |i| puts i }

#=>
1
2
3
4
5
```

Similarly, we may need to increment by an alternative iterator (say 2 rather than 1), we can therefore use the step iterator that accepts 2 parameters. The first parameter is the same as the upto iterator, the maximum number that the iterator should loop up to, and secondly the step that should be incremented each time.

```
#!/usr/bin/env ruby
1.step(10,2) { |i| puts i }

#=>
1
3
5
7
9
```

Each_Index Iterator

There are times, most normally when we are debugging some unusual behavior, that we need to loop through an array, but we are only interested in the index of an array, rather than the actual value held within the array. For this we can use the each_index iterator, which works the same way as the each iterator.

```
#!/usr/bin/env ruby
vals = [5,10,15,20,25,30,35,40]
vals.each_index { |i| puts "#{i} = #{vals[i]}" }

#=>
0 = 5
1 = 10
2 = 15
3 = 20
4 = 25
5 = 30
6 = 35
7 = 40
```

Very early on in this chapter we discussed the redo keyword during the while and until loops. We have an alternative available for use within the for loop, and the iterators discussed later in the chapter. Whereas the redo keyword restarts the running of the block, the retry keyword re-evaluates the initial condition, before looping once more. This is ideal when you have a check within a loop that you require to run one further time if another condition is met.

Exercise

We can now apply a number of the previous loops and iterators back in to our initial example exercise to pick suitable DVDs to watch. We initially create three arrays. One will contain the full list of DVDs, and as we drill down further into the criteria we will set a new array to contain the suitable values.

Initially we use the each iterator, which as discussed within this chapter is perfect for looping through an array, to drill down any films with the certification between a 10 and 15.

Finally, we use the while loop, to loop *X* number of times (the selected_dvd's variable's count) and check that the timing of the film is suitable before adding this film to the final array.

We then use an until loop to loop through until all the suitable DVDs have been output onto the screen.

```ruby
#!/usr/bin/env ruby

dvds = Array.new
selected_dvds = Array.new
final_dvds = Array.new

dvds.push([100000,137,"Skyfall",12])
dvds.push([100001,114,"The Hurt Locker",15])
dvds.push([100002,105,"21 Jump Street",15])
dvds.push([100003,100,"Finding Nemo",'U'])

dvds.each { |item|
        if item[3].to_i.between?(10,15)
                selected_dvds.push(item)
        end
}

i = 0
while i < selected_dvds.count
        if selected_dvds[i][1].quo(60).to_f < 2
                final_dvds.push(selected_dvds[i])
        end
        i+=1
end

i = 0
until i == final_dvds.count
        print "\aYAY! We can watch ", final_dvds[i][2], "\n"
        i+=1
end

#=>
YAY! We can watch The Hurt Locker
YAY! We can watch 21 Jump Street
```

CHAPTER 10

■ ■ ■

Functions and Methods

We have learned a lot about the Ruby programming language itself in the previous chapters along with its syntax and type characteristics. In this chapter we begin to look at "reusable code," the ability to write a snippet of code that can be used multiple times during our application. This is sometimes known as the D.R.Y. (Don't Repeat Yourself) principle.

Technically, because Ruby is a fully object-oriented language, Ruby's functions are actually all methods, as they are all linked to objects.

Defining and Calling Methods

To call our Hello World multiple times, we will write a simple method named hello, and will call this once defined:

```ruby
#!/usr/bin/env ruby
def hello
    puts "Hello World"
end

hello

#=>
Hello World
```

As Ruby can also accept parameters to methods, we can use the alternative syntax when calling the method such as hello():

```ruby
#!/usr/bin/env ruby
def hello
    puts "Hello World"
end

hello()

#=>
Hello World
```

Now that we have said "Hello" to the whole world, we will personalize this method by enhancing it to accept a method, of the name of the user, and the method will say "Hello" directly to the user.

```ruby
#!/usr/bin/env ruby
def hello(name)
    puts "Hello #{name}"
end

hello('Matt')

#=>
Hello Matt
```

Default Parameters

As with many other programming languages, we can enhance the method further to hold a "default" value, so that we can overload the function. If the function has no parameters passed (such as the first call to hello) this will take the default value. If we pass a parameter, this will be used instead.

```ruby
#!/usr/bin/env ruby
def hello(name = "World")
    puts "Hello #{name}"
end

hello
hello()
hello('Matt')
hello 'Matt'

#=>
Hello World
Hello World
Hello Matt
Hello Matt
```

You will notice in the preceding examples that the parameter brackets are completely optional, even when passing in parameters.

Initialize Method

As with many other programming languages, Ruby has an initialize method, similar to PHP's __construct method. When writing a class, we can supply multiple methods that can interact with each other, including the initialize method, which is run on creating an object of the class.

```ruby
#!/usr/bin/env ruby
class ClockInMachine
        def initialize(name)
                @name = name
        end
        def clock_in
                puts "Welcome #{@name}"
        end
        def clock_out
                puts "Goodbye #{@name}, see you tomorrow"
        end
end

clock_in_machine = ClockInMachine.new "Matt"
clock_in_machine.clock_in
clock_in_machine.clock_out

#=>
Welcome Matt
Goodbye Matt, see you tomorrow
```

Returns

All the methods we have shown here have highlighted how we can write code once, and use it multiple times, however the previous examples are an "endpoint" method, meaning they do not pass on anything useful further. We can instead make our methods return a value, instead of outputting it, which can then be used elsewhere.

```ruby
#!/usr/bin/env ruby
def hello
        "Hello World"
end

hello
puts hello

#=>
Hello World
```

You will notice that we called the hello method twice, once we just called the method that returned Hello World, but we didn't do anything with the return. When we called the method for the second time we actually used the return by passing this to puts.

You will also notice that we just state "Hello World" without actually stating to return this. In Ruby the last statement will always be returned, unless a return statement is called before as shown here:

```ruby
#!/usr/bin/env ruby
def hello
    return "Hello Matt"
    "Hello World"
end

puts hello

#=>
Hello Matt
```

Returning Multiple Values

We can also extend our returns to return multiple pieces of data if required as follows:

```ruby
#!/usr/bin/env ruby
def return_multiple
    k = 10
    l = 20
    m = 4
    return k, l, m
end

puts return_multiple

#=>
10
20
4
```

Complex Methods

We have previously shown how methods can be used for very simple logic, by passing in a (optional) first parameter or no parameters at all. We can advance this further to compute more complex problems.

```ruby
#!/usr/bin/env ruby
def addition(num1, num2)
    num1 + num2
end
```

```ruby
puts addition 1, 4
puts addition 5, 382

#=>
5
387
```

We can also have functions calling other functions if required.

```ruby
#!/usr/bin/env ruby
def addition(num1, num2)
    num1 + num2
end

def minus(num1, num2)
    num1 - num2
end

def times(num1, num2)
    num1 * num2
end

def divide(num1, num2)
    num1 / num2
end

def calculate(type, num1, num2)
    if type == 'add'
        return addition num1, num2
    elsif type == 'minus'
        return minus num1, num2
    elsif type == 'times'
        return times num1, num2
    elsif type == 'divide'
        return divide num1, num2
    end

    "Error"
end

puts calculate 'add', 1, 4
puts calculate 'times', 5, 382
puts calculate 'modulus', 5, 3
puts calculate 'divide', 90, 9

#=>
5
1910
Error
10
```

Named and Variable Parameters

The only issue with what we have written previously, is that while we can supply default parameters for a method, if we say we want to change the last parameter; we still have to provide all parameters as follows:

```ruby
#!/usr/bin/env ruby
def really_long_maths(num1 = 2, num2 = 2, num3 = 3, num4 = 8, num5 = 1)
    num1 * num2 - num3 + num4 / num5
end

puts really_long_maths
puts really_long_maths 2, 2, 3, 8, 2

#=>
9
5
```

Notice that in the second example, we only wanted to change the last parameter. However we had to supply all other parameters default values just to be able to do this. There is a better way! We can utilize a hash being passed in, and supply some default values within this hash if the key is not provided.

```ruby
#!/usr/bin/env ruby
def really_long_maths(opts={})
    params = {
        :num1 => 2,
        :num2 => 2,
        :num3 => 3,
        :num4 => 8,
        :num5 => 1
    }.merge(opts)

    params[:num1] * params[:num2] - params[:num3] + params[:num4] /
params[:num5]
end

puts really_long_maths
puts really_long_maths( :num5 => 2 )
puts really_long_maths({ :num3 => 6, :num5 => 2 })

#=>
9
5
2
```

Notice that we merge our options hash into a hash of default parameters. This way we only need to supply the parameters that we want to change.

We can also allow a variable number of parameters to be passed in, and loop through these if required.

```
#!/usr/bin/env ruby
def my_pets(*pets)
    puts "I have #{pets.count} types of pet"
    for i in 0...pets.length
        puts "I have a #{pets[i]}"
    end
end

my_pets "Dog", "Cat", "Horse", "Praying Mantis"
puts "-------------"
my_pets "Fish", "Owl"

#=>
I have 4 types of pet
I have a Dog
I have a Cat
I have a Horse
I have a Praying Mantis
-------------
I have 2 types of pet
I have a Fish
I have a Owl
```

Starting with Ruby 2.0, we can now pass "real" named parameters into a function, without having to resort to a hash to cater for this.

```
#!/usr/bin/env ruby
def my_name(first_name: "Joe", last_name: "Bloggs")
  puts "#{first_name} #{last_name}"
end

my_name(first_name: "Matt")

#=>
Matt Bloggs
```

Aliasing a Method

Within Ruby we can alias a method if required. To do this, we use the syntax

```
alias <<new name>> <<current method name>>

#!/usr/bin/env ruby
def hello
    puts "Hello World"
end

alias welcome hello

hello
welcome

#=>
Hello World
Hello World
```

Un-defining a Method

We may require the ability to un-define a method, or alias of a method on occasions. Ruby supports this by using the undef syntax as follows:

```
undef <<method name or alias name>>

#!/usr/bin/env ruby
def hello
    puts "Hello World"
end

alias welcome hello

undef hello

welcome
hello

#=>
Hello World
fig14.rb:11:in `<main>': undefined local variable or method `hello' for
main:Object (NameError)
```

Class Methods versus Instance Methods

We have shown a number of examples of "instance methods" previously, whereby we address the instance of a class, rather than a class itself.

```ruby
#!/usr/bin/env ruby
class Car
  def self.hello
    puts "Hello from the Car Class"
  end
  def hello
    puts "Hello from My Car"
  end
end

Car.hello
Car.new.hello

#=>
Hello from the Car Class
Hello from My Car
```

Exercise

Now that we have methods in our knowledgebase, we can make the DVD exercise much simpler and more reusable.

We initially declare our three methods, which each run a piece of the processing. The first two methods are used for filtering, and use the Ruby 2.0 named parameter syntax to set default values. These methods simply return a reduced array, which is then passed to the next function in turn. The last function simply iterates through the remaining array and outputs the films that we can watch.

We declare the dvds parameter as Array.new if one is not passed, so that an array can be returned.

```ruby
#!/usr/bin/env ruby

def age_check(min_age: 10, max_age: 15, dvds: Array.new)
    dvds.keep_if { |item| item[3].to_i.between?(10,15) }
end

def length_check(max_hours: 2, max_minutes: 0, dvds: Array.new)
    max_num_of_minutes = (max_hours*60) + max_minutes
    dvds.keep_if { |item| item[1].to_i < max_num_of_minutes }
end
```

```ruby
def what_can_we_watch(dvds)
    dvds.each {|dvd| print "\aYAY! We can watch ", dvd[2], "\n" }
end

dvds = Array.new
selected_dvds = Array.new
final_dvds = Array.new

dvds.push([100000,137,"Skyfall",12])
dvds.push([100001,114,"The Hurt Locker",15])
dvds.push([100002,105,"21 Jump Street",15])
dvds.push([100003,100,"Finding Nemo",'U'])

selected_dvds = age_check(dvds: dvds)

final_dvds = length_check(dvds: selected_dvds)

what_can_we_watch(final_dvds)

#=>
YAY! We can watch The Hurt Locker
YAY! We can watch 21 Jump Street
```

CHAPTER 11

■ ■ ■

Classes and Modules

In the previous chapters we have discussed the basics of the Ruby programming language, without looking at it from an object- oriented point of view. Object orientation is an alternative to the procedural method of programming. Procedural code runs from top to bottom in a very simple and linear way. Object-oriented programming includes creating a set of classes, with associated methods (such as a class called Car, with a method called startEngine). We then initialize these classes by creating instance objects of the class in order to call the method.

```ruby
#!/usr/bin/env ruby

class Car
  def startEngine
    puts "Engine Started"
  end
end

my_car = Car.new
my_car.startEngine

#=>
Engine Started
```

Properties

We can extend our classes to support properties; the getting and setting of variables within a class so that the object as can access these as required, within different methods. To do so, rather like other programming languages, we create getter and setter methods, which get the variable and set the variable, respectively.

```ruby
#!/usr/bin/env ruby

class Car
  def getColour
    @colour
  end

  def setColour colour
    @colour = colour
  end

end

my_car = Car.new
my_car.setColour "Blue"

puts "My Car is #{my_car.getColour}"

#=>
My Car is Blue
```

We can enhance this further, by instead using a method to setColour, and one to getColour—we can set property setting. This means that we can set a variable within a class, the same way that you would set an internal variable. Notice the def colour= colour (without the space) that allows a property to become accessible at a class level.

```ruby
#!/usr/bin/env ruby

class Car
  def colour
    @colour
  end

  def colour= colour
    @colour = colour
  end

end

my_car = Car.new
my_car.colour = "Blue"

puts "My Car is #{my_car.colour}"

#=>
My Car is Blue
```

While this kind of functionality exists within many other programming languages, Ruby provides us with the attr_accessor method, which allows us to set properties that can be updated at an object level, without having to produce any code as we had to previously.

```ruby
#!/usr/bin/env ruby

class Car
  attr_accessor :colour, :engine_size
end

my_car = Car.new

my_car.colour = "Red"
puts my_car.colour

my_car.engine_size = 1400
puts my_car.engine_size

#=>
Red
1400
```

While we have used the attr_accessor statement previously (which allows read and write access to the properties named) we can use attr_reader to define properties that we can read-only; and attr_writer to define properties that we can write to, but not read from.

Constructors

Ruby provides us with the capability to create a constructor method, one that is called when an object of a class is initialized. This allows some default properties to be set, or some setup code to be executed before the object is used.

```ruby
#!/usr/bin/env ruby

class Vehicle
  def initialize (colour, engine_size, type = 'Car')
    @colour = colour
    @engine_size = engine_size
    @type = type
  end
end

my_car = Vehicle.new("Blue",1400)
hire_van = Vehicle.new("While",2200,"Van")
```

Private Methods

Ruby allows us to create private methods, which external calls cannot access. Only internal methods can call these private methods (an internal method meaning a method within the same class).

```ruby
#!/usr/bin/env ruby

class Car
  def showEngineSize
    puts getEngineSize
  end

  private

  def getEngineSize
    1400
  end

end

my_car = Car.new

my_car.showEngineSize

my_car.getEngineSize

#=>
1400
fig05.rb:20:in `<main>': private method `getEngineSize' called for
#<Car:0x00000101089b00> (NoMethodError)
```

Protected Methods

A private method can only be called by its own object, protected methods allow an object to access other objects of the same class's methods.

```ruby
#!/usr/bin/env ruby

class Car
  attr_accessor :colour

  protected :colour

  def <=>(other_car)
    colour <=> other_car.colour
  end
end
```

```
my_car = Car.new
my_car.colour = "Red"

hire_car = Car.new
hire_car.colour = "Blue"

puts my_car == hire_car
puts my_car != hire_car

#=>
false
true
```

Modules

Within other programming languages you have namespaces; Ruby groups classes together in namespaces by using modules to group a set of classes.

```
#!/usr/bin/env ruby

module Vehicle
  class Car
    def hello
      puts "I am a car"
    end
  end

  class Van
    def hello
      puts "I am a van"
    end
  end
end

include Vehicle

my_car = Car.new
my_car.hello

#=>
I am a car
```

We could also drop the use of `include`, which will include the module required, and statically include this in our initialization of objects.

```ruby
#!/usr/bin/env ruby

module Vehicle
  class Car
    def hello
      puts "I am a car"
    end
  end

  class Van
    def hello
      puts "I am a van"
    end
  end
end

my_car = Vehicle::Car.new
my_car.hello

#=>
I am a car
```

In the previous section we have demonstrated using modules for object-oriented programming, Modules exist simply to group together a set of reusable code. Working back previous to OOP, we could simply group together a set of functions if required.

```ruby
#!/usr/bin/env ruby

module Maths
  def self.add num1, num2
    num1 + num2
  end

  def self.minus num1, num2
    num1 - num2
  end
end

puts Maths.add 20, 5

puts Maths.minus 131, 32

#=>
25
99
```

Ruby Class Variables

Within Ruby, we have a number of types of variables available to us, especially when working with object-oriented programming. It is worth understanding (and remembering) the various syntaxes to these to avoid complex debugging when trying to establish why a variable is not holding its value as expected.

Local Variables

Local variables are our "normal variables" that are set within a method in Ruby, and no other method/call can access these variables at any time. Local variables normally start with a lowercase letter or an underscore.

```ruby
#!/usr/bin/env ruby
class Car
  def engine_size engine_size
    engine_size_display = engine_size/1000

    puts "Engine Size is #{engine_size_display}L"
  end
end

my_car = Car.new
my_car.engine_size 2000
#=>
Engine Size is 2L
```

Instance Variables

Instance variables are available within any method of an instance or object. This means that the variables can be accessed and updated across various methods, rather like we demonstrated previously within the getter/setter example. Instance variables are preceded by the at sign (@) followed by the variable name.

```ruby
#!/usr/bin/env ruby
class Car
  def engine_size
    puts "Engine Size is #{@engine_size_display}L"
  end
  def engine_size= engine_size
    @engine_size_display = engine_size/1000
  end
end

my_car = Car.new
my_car.engine_size = 2000
my_car.engine_size
#=>
Engine Size is 2L
```

89

Class Variable

A Class variable is accessible across different objects of the same class. This is a characteristic of the class, and belongs to the class. These variables start with a double at sign (@@) followed by the variable name.

```ruby
#!/usr/bin/env ruby
class Car
  def initialize
    @@broken = false
  end

  def set_broken
    @@broken = true
  end

  def get_broken
    @@broken
  end
end

my_car = Car.new
new_car = Car.new

puts new_car.get_broken
my_car.set_broken
puts new_car.get_broken
#=>
false
true
```

Global Variable

A Global variable is available across various classes, and all calling code. These are preceded by the dollar sign ($).

```ruby
#!/usr/bin/env ruby

$version_number = '1.2.1'

class MyCode
  def get_version
    puts "Current Code is Version: #{$version_number}"
  end
end
```

```ruby
class Release
  def set_new_version(version_number)
    $version_number = version_number
  end
end

my_code = MyCode.new
release = Release.new

my_code.get_version
release.set_new_version '1.2.2'
my_code.get_version

#=>
Current Code is Version: 1.2.1
Current Code is Version: 1.2.2
```

CHAPTER 12

■ ■ ■

Blocks, Procs, and Lambdas

Some of the most powerful features of the Ruby language are closures, which are known as blocks, procs, and lambdas within Ruby. Closures within Ruby are also often misunderstood, mainly due to the flexibility when using them within Ruby.

A *closure* is in essence a function that can be stored as a variable; closures within Ruby are mainly used for iterating through data/result sets. Closures allow external access to local variables from within the closure.

Blocks

The simplest of the three closures is a block; this follows Ruby's "normal" programming style. Blocks are simply "bits" of code that can be executed.

Ruby blocks follow either the do..end syntax, or curly braces {} and often combine methods such as each, times, and collect to iterate through each element of a hash or array.

```ruby
#!/usr/bin/env ruby
[1, 2, 3, 4].each do |n|
        puts n
end

#=>
1
2
3
4
```

```ruby
#!/usr/bin/env ruby
[1, 2, 3].each { |n| puts n }

#=>
1
2
3
```

Likewise, we can use the `times` method to execute the block a set number of times.

```ruby
#!/usr/bin/env ruby
3.times { |i| puts "Hello!" }
#=>
Hello!
Hello!
Hello!
```

We mentioned the `collect` method previously, which is one of the most useful methods when dealing with blocks. The `collect` method applies the block to each element within an array provided.

```ruby
#!/usr/bin/env ruby
scores = [10, 8, 5]
puts scores.collect { |score| score + 1 }

puts scores

#=>
11
9
6
10
8
5
```

You will notice that within the block, using the `collect` method, we increased the score by 1, and outputting the results from this statement displayed the updated scores. You will also notice that when we output the contents of the scores array, these were unchanged.

As outlined in earlier chapters, we can append an exclamation mark to the `collect` method, (`collect!`), which will store the outcomes of the block back to the original array.

```ruby
#!/usr/bin/env ruby
scores = [10, 8, 5]
puts scores.collect! { |score| score + 1 }

puts scores
#=>
11
9
6
11
9
6
```

Yield

Using a yield statement we can pass control between a method and a block, and back again as required. To utilize this, we simply create a function and a block with the same name and then use the yield statement to call the block when required.

```ruby
#!/usr/bin/env ruby

def hello
        puts "In the Method"
        yield
        puts "Back in the Method"
        yield
end

hello { puts "You are in the block" }

#=>
In the Method
You are in the block
Back in the Method
You are in the block
```

We can enhance the preceding code to support parameters being passed in:

```ruby
#!/usr/bin/env ruby

def hello
        puts "Hello Person"
        yield "Joe"
        puts "Hello Person"
        yield "Peter"
end

hello { |name| puts "Hello #{name}" }

#=>
Hello Person
Hello Joe
Hello Person
Hello Peter
```

Blocks can also support multiple parameters, even when being called via the yield statement. To do this you simply call yield param1, param2:

```ruby
#!/usr/bin/env ruby

def hello
        puts "Hello Person"
        yield "Joe", "Bloggs"
        puts "Hello Person"
        yield "Peter", "Crouch"
end

hello { |first_name,last_name| puts "Hello #{first_name} #{last_name}" }

#=>
Hello Person
Hello Joe Bloggs
Hello Person
Hello Peter Crouch
```

Procs

The main issue with a block is that the code is simply runnable, but cannot be stored to a variable to be run in multiple places like a method. Therefore the code is not reusable across our application. A *proc* is simply a block that can be stored to a variable, and executed from multiple places across our application.

```ruby
#!/usr/bin/env ruby
times_two = Proc.new do |n|
  n * 2
end

puts (1..20).to_a.collect(&times_two).inspect

#=>
[2, 4, 6, 8, 10, 12, 14, 16, 18, 20, 22, 24, 26, 28, 30, 32, 34, 36, 38, 40]
```

Procs are very simple to write, and simply require you to define Proc.new and assign this to a variable; other than they work similarly to a block. Also, we need to convert the proc into a block for methods such as the collect and map methods; which is why we specify the &proc_name syntax shown previously. (Note that the map and collect methods do exactly the same thing.)

```ruby
#!/usr/bin/env ruby
square = Proc.new { |x| x ** 2 }

puts [1, 2, 3, 4, 5].collect!(&square).inspect
puts [1, 2, 3, 4, 5].map!(&square).inspect

#=>
[1, 4, 9, 16, 25]
[1, 4, 9, 16, 25]
```

In the previous example we converted our proc back to a block in order to execute it. We can instead use the proc_name.call syntax to call the proc directly.

```ruby
#!/usr/bin/env ruby
test_proc = Proc.new { puts "Hello World" }

test_proc.call

#=>
Hello World
```

Lambdas

A *lambda* is almost identical to a proc, just with an alternative syntax. Rather than using the Proc.new syntax, we define a lambda using the lamba keyword

```ruby
#!/usr/bin/env ruby

def lambda_test(my_lambda)
  puts "Method here!"
  my_lambda.call
end

lambda_test(lambda { puts "Lambda here!" })

#=>
Method here!
Lambda here!
```

Here we are defining a method called lambda_test, and accepting a parameter of my_lambda, which will run some code within the method itself, before running the lambda passed in. Within the call to our method, we are defining a lambda.

Here we simplify this process further, by removing the method from the code example to outline how we define a lambda, and passing an array of names to the lambda (which we convert to a block as per our proc example):

```ruby
#!/usr/bin/env ruby
output = lambda { |name| puts name }

names = ["Joe", "Paul", "Peter", "John"]

names.collect(&output)

#=>
Joe
Paul
Peter
John
```

Although procs and lambdas are almost identical, there are a few minor differences in the way that they function that are worth noting at this stage.

First, a lambda checks the number of parameters passed in, and will throw an error if an invalid number of parameters are passed in, whereas a proc will just treat all missing parameters as nil values.

Second, when a lambda returns, it passes control back to the calling method, whereas a proc instantly returns without passing back control to the calling method.

```ruby
def villain_superhero_proc
  winner = Proc.new { return "Villain Wins!" }
  winner.call
  "Superhero Wins!"
end

puts villain_superhero_proc

def villain_superhero_lambda
  winner = lambda { return "Villain Wins!" }
  winner.call
  "Superhero Wins!"
end

puts villain_superhero_lambda

#=>
Villain Wins!
Superhero Wins!
```

You will notice here, that in the proc example, the execution stops after calling the proc method as the return, passing control directly back to the calling statement rather than the internal proc; whereas the Lambda returns to the internal method, which then itself returns further on.

EXERCISE

We can adapt our original exercise of the DVD sorter to use blocks, procs and lambdas instead.

We utilize a lambda for our initial check, which returns the original DVD array if the rating is between a 10 and 15, or else this returns nil (which we then strip out using the compact method), before storing this as the array `selected_dvds`.

We then pass this array through a proc, which checks that the DVD's length is less than 2 hours, again returning the DVD array if this passes, or nil if this fails. However we use the `collect!` call for this, so this updates our `selected_dvds` array.

Finally we utilize a block to pass each of the selected DVDs through, which outputs the DVDs that we can watch.

```ruby
#!/usr/bin/env ruby

length_check = Proc.new do |dvd|
   if(dvd[1].to_i < 120)
      dvd
   else
     nil
   end
end

age_check = lambda { |dvd| (dvd[3].to_i.between?(10,15) ? dvd : nil)
}

dvds = Array.new
dvds.push([100000,137,"Skyfall",12])
dvds.push([100001,114,"The Hurt Locker",15])
dvds.push([100002,105,"21 Jump Street",15])
dvds.push([100003,100,"Finding Nemo",'U'])

selected_dvds = dvds.map(&age_check).compact

selected_dvds.collect!(&length_check)

selected_dvds.compact.each { |dvd| print "\aYAY! We can watch ",
dvd[2], "\n" }

#=>
YAY! We can watch The Hurt Locker
YAY! We can watch 21 Jump Street
```

CHAPTER 13

∎ ∎ ∎

Errors and Exceptions

Within Ruby, as well in almost all other object-oriented and procedural-based programming languages, we have the option to throw and handle errors and exceptions within our code. Some of these errors and exceptions we will want to generate ourselves, such as when we have detected some abnormal behavior within the system, whereas other errors and exceptions will be thrown from the Ruby language itself, or other third-party libraries.

For example, we have built a system that allows some text and a photo to be uploaded to an external service (for example, Twitter). We will want to throw our own errors if the user's message is too long for the service, but likewise we will want to handle a network or communications error that Ruby will throw if we fail to connect to this external service.

In Ruby, an error is thrown by the means of an exception, which can be handled by catching or raising the error.

Errors

Ruby errors are simply child classes of the StandardError class that is part of the Ruby core classes. We can use a small snippet of Ruby code to loop through the StandardErrors within Ruby and output these in a hierarchical structure. Some of the more common error codes within Ruby (based upon version 2.1.2) are shown here:

Error Name	Meaning (From Ruby Documentation)
NoMemoryError	Raised when memory allocation fails.
Gem::LoadError	Raised when RubyGems is unable to load or activate a gem. Contains the name and version requirements of the gem that either conflicts with already activated gems or that RubyGems is otherwise unable to activate.
NotImplementedError	Raised when a feature is not implemented on the current platform. For example, methods depending on the fsync or fork system calls may raise this exception if the underlying operating system or Ruby runtime does not support them.

(continued)

101

Error Name	Meaning (From Ruby Documentation)
SecurityError	Raised when attempting a potential unsafe operation, typically when the $SAFE level is raised above 0.
Interrupt	Raised with the interrupt signal is received, typically because the user pressed on Control-C (on most posix platforms). As such, it is a subclass of SignalException.
ThreadError	Raised when an invalid operation is attempted on a thread.
TypeError	Raised when encountering an object that is not of the expected type. [1, 2, 3].first("two") #=> TypeError: no implicit conversion of String into Integer
ZeroDivisionError	Raised when attempting to divide an integer by 0. 42 / 0 #=> ZeroDivisionError: divided by 0

In Ruby 2.1.2 there are over 150 different types of errors that can be thrown.

Catching Errors and Exceptions

Within Ruby, we will often need to catch errors, so that the raw error is not displayed back to the user; to do this we use the rescue syntax:

Unhandled Error:

```
#!/usr/bin/env ruby
begin
  puts 1/0
end

#=>
fig01.rb:3:in `/': divided by 0 (ZeroDivisionError)
    from fig01.rb:3:in `<main>'
```

Handled Error:

```
#!/usr/bin/env ruby
begin
  puts 1/0
rescue
  puts "Sorry, we can't divide by Zero"
end

#=>
Sorry, we can't divide by Zero
```

We have now correctly handled an error, and displayed a more user-friendly message instead. However by simply stating rescue we have started to handle all errors thrown within this code. The same code syntax with just the added ability to pull through the type of error being thrown, and throwing a different error above (the file does not exist) will output as follows:

```ruby
#!/usr/bin/env ruby
begin
  file = File.open("file_not_here.txt")
  puts 1/0
rescue StandardError => error
  puts "Sorry, we can't divide by Zero"
  puts "Error actually thrown is #{error.class}"
end
end

#=>
Sorry, we can't divide by Zero
Error actually thrown is Errno::ENOENT
```

Notice that as we handled all errors, we displayed an error message stating that we can't divide by Zero when the actual error was due to an invalid file attempting to be opened.

We can improve these error handlings, by handling the actual errors we want to handle, and doing something useful with them, such as throwing more reasonable error messages.

```ruby
#!/usr/bin/env ruby
begin
  file = File.open("file_not_here.txt")
  puts 1/0
rescue ZeroDivisionError => error
  puts "Sorry, we can't divide by Zero"
  puts "Error: #{error.to_s}"
rescue Errno::ENOENT => error
  puts "Sorry, we can't open the file requested"
  puts "Error: #{error.to_s}"
end

#=>
Sorry, we can't open the file requested
Error: No such file or directory @ rb_sysopen - file_not_here.txt
```

Raising Exceptions

Raising an exception within Ruby is very similar to throwing/catching errors in most
other programming languages; this often confuses new developers working with Ruby, as
they attempt to create some throw/catch statements, which work very differently in Ruby.
Therefore we use the raise/rescue syntax the same way in Ruby as we would use
a throw/catch in other languages such as C#.

```
#!/usr/bin/env ruby
begin
  raise 'Testing an Exception'
  puts "Shouldn't execute this code"
rescue Exception => error
  puts "Rescued an Exception: #{error.inspect}"
end

#=>
Rescued an Exception: #<RuntimeError: Testing an Exception>
```

Here we have just thrown a RuntimeError as we did not specify the type of exception
that we wanted to raise. We can pass in an initial parameter when calling raise to specify
the exception type, followed by the message we want to raise.

```
#!/usr/bin/env ruby
begin
  raise ZeroDivisionError, 'My fake ZeroDivisionError'
  puts "Shouldn't execute this code"
rescue Exception => error
  puts "Rescued an Exception: #{error.inspect}"
end

#=>
Rescued an Exception: #<ZeroDivisionError: My fake ZeroDivisionError>
```

When an error or exception is thrown within Ruby, this terminates the running of the
block currently being executed (like a try/catch block in other programming languages).
We can however allow continuation of our application by continuing with statements
outside of the block.

```
#!/usr/bin/env ruby
begin
  raise ZeroDivisionError, 'My fake ZeroDivisionError'
  puts "Shouldn't execute this code"
rescue Exception => error
  puts "Rescued an Exception: #{error.inspect}"
end
```

Creating Our Own Exceptions

As shown in the previous examples, we can raise generic exceptions within our code when an unexpected scenario occurs, however are not always easily identifiable as to the reason that a particular scenario occurred. Therefore if we rescue the standard errors it is not guaranteed that the exception was raised for the reason that we intended. Instead we can define our own exceptions, and raise these so that we have a better idea as to what has happened within our application.

```ruby
#!/usr/bin/env ruby
class MyTestException < StandardError
end

begin
  raise MyTestException
rescue MyTestException => error
  puts "Rescued an Exception: #{error.inspect}"
end

#=>
Rescued an Exception: #<MyTestException: MyTestException>
```

Like with standard Exceptions, we can also pass a message over to the exception, so that this can be retrieved when caught within the rescue statement. Passing messages to an exception are particularly useful for debugging purposes; such as logging exceptions that have been thrown, as this can provide additional information about why the exception was thrown.

```ruby
#!/usr/bin/env ruby
class MyTestException < StandardError
end

begin
  raise MyTestException, 'Hello'
rescue MyTestException => error
  puts "Rescued an Exception: #{error.inspect}"
end

#=>
Rescued an Exception: #<MyTestException: Hello>
```

We can also output the backtrace of the exception, which details further how the exception was thrown, and which sections of code the exception had been generated from.

```ruby
#!/usr/bin/env ruby
def testing_block
  begin
    raise Exception
  rescue Exception => error
    puts error.backtrace.inspect
  end
end

testing_block

#=>
["fig11.rb:4:in `testing_block'", "fig11.rb:10:in `<main>'"]
```

Ensure

In other object-oriented programming languages we have the finally statement that
always executes after a try/catch block has been completed—regardless of whether the
statement exited normally, or with an exception. Similarly in Ruby we can use the ensure
statement for this.

```ruby
#!/usr/bin/env ruby
begin
  puts "Hello"
  raise Exception
  puts "Hello Again"
rescue Exception => error
  puts "Rescued an Exception"
ensure
  puts "Goodbye!"
end

#=>
Hello
Rescued an Exception
Goodbye!
```

The ensure statement is very useful for handling both the successful results and
unsuccessful results of a statement, such as a database update. We could use the main
block to run a query, and raise an exception if something unordinary occurred. We can
roll-back our changes within the rescue statement, and report the error back to the user;
before closing and disconnecting from the database regardless of the outcome during the
ensure statement.

Throw/Catch

While Ruby utilizes the raise/rescue syntax for throwing and catching exceptions, it still has the throw and catch keywords that can be utilized for a similar purposes, but are not directly linked to handling exceptions.

The throw/catch syntax within Ruby is similar to a break statement within other programming languages, as follows:

```
#!/usr/bin/env ruby
catch :test_throw_catch do
  puts "Here I Am"
  throw :test_throw_catch
  puts "Hello"
end

#=>
Here I Am
```

We can utilize this further within a loop that allows the loop to exit once a certain scenario passes.

```
#!/usr/bin/env ruby
catch :quit_loop do
  1000000.times do |i|
    throw :quit_loop if i > 10
    puts i
  end
end

puts "Ok, we're done!"

#=>
0
1
2
3
4
5
6
7
8
9
10
Ok, we're done!
```

CHAPTER 14

■ ■ ■

Input/Output

Input/Output within Ruby is the ability to bi-directionally communicate between Ruby and an external resource, such as a file or network resource. It is worth noting that Input/Output is not just restricted to File processes, as often wrongly assumed. Ruby Input/Output is defined from the single base class IO. Derived from the IO class, we then have more specialized, but otherwise similar subclasses, such as File and BasicSocket that deal with the Input/Output for the particular type of resource.

Previously, we have dealt with Standard Input/Output, which allows us to communicate interactively with the user running our Ruby application. We can output text to the screen for the user to view, and we can prompt the user to enter some information back into our application that we can interpret.

```
#!/usr/bin/env ruby
puts "Hello there, please can you enter your name"

name = gets
puts "Hello #{name}"

#=>
Hello there, please can you enter your name
Matt
Hello Matt
```

Note that I entered Matt when the application ran, and prompted for user input.

In addition to the gets and puts methods, we have additional Standard Input/Output methods available to us, the most common of which are detailed here:

Method Name	Purpose

gets	Gets the user input until the return key is fired. Note that this also captures the new line into the variable. We can also use the chomp method to trim this string down from new lines.
	
	``ruby
	#!/usr/bin/env ruby
	name = gets
	puts "Hello #{name}, welcome!"
	
	puts ""
	
	name = gets.chomp
	puts "Hello #{name}, welcome!"
	
	#=>
	Matt
	Hello Matt
	, welcome!
	
	Matt
	Hello Matt, welcome!
	``

puts	Puts the string passed in onto the output display, followed by a new line.
open	Opens the resource passed in to the function. This can be a resource or file and the kernel will work out how to open this file/resource.
print	Puts the string passed in onto the output display; however no new line is output after the string.

printf	Interprets the string passed in (including any placeholder values), and outputs the modified string:
	
	``ruby
	#!/usr/bin/env ruby
	name = gets.chomp
	printf("Hello %s\n",name)
	
	#=>
	Matt
	Hello Matt
	``

(continued)

110

Method Name	Purpose
putc	Works similar to puts; however allows a single character to be output rather than a string: ```#!/usr/bin/env ruby\nstr = "ABCDEFGH"\nputc str\n#=>\nA```
readline	Allows the reading of a single line from a File/Resource Handle or Standard Input.
readlines	Reads a file, and splits the new lines into elements within an array for Ruby to iterate through.

File Input/Output

The most commonly used method of Input/Output within Ruby is when dealing with files being input or output. This is where the Ruby interpreter opens a file handle (opening an existing or new file) and read or writes some data from this file. This is particularly useful when writing log files, reading configuration files, or general reading or writing to files for application purposes.

To start with, we will simply open and close a file handle on a file, which we could then read if required between the opening and closing of the file handle.

```
#!/usr/bin/env ruby
file = File.open("test.txt","r")

#Do some "stuff" with a Text File

file.close
#=>
fig05.rb:2:in `initialize': No such file or directory
@ rb_sysopen - test.txt (Errno::ENOENT)
        from fig05.rb:2:in `open'
        from fig05.rb:2:in `<main>'
```

Here, we didn't create the file test.txt before running our application, as we are attempting to read the file; and it does not exist, we receive this warning. We can create the file initially, and then re-run our application:

```
touch test.txt
ruby fig05.rb
#=>
```

Note that we receive no output, but receive no error either; this is because we are simply opening a file for reading, then closing the file without doing anything. Instead we can now read data from the file, and output it on the screen:

```
#!/usr/bin/env ruby
file = File.open("test2.txt","r")
puts file.inspect
puts file.read
file.close

#=>
#<File:test2.txt>
Hello World from my file!!
```

You can see from this code that we are now inspecting the file handle, which simply reports on details regarding the file handle, such as the filename that is opened. Then we output the file.read method that reads the entire file's content and we simply output this.

We will now create a text file containing the following content, and attempt to just read a single line from the file using the readline method.

```
Hello World from my file!!

Testing 123
```

```
#!/usr/bin/env ruby
file = File.open("test3.txt","r")
puts file.inspect
puts file.readline
file.close

#=>
#<File:test3.txt>
Hello World from my file!!
```

While this doesn't seem particularly useful at this stage, we could combine the readline method with a loop through each line of the file, and process each line of the file.

```
#!/usr/bin/env ruby
file = File.open("shopping_list.txt","r")
while(item = file.readline) != nil
  puts "We need to buy #{item.chomp} today."
end
file.close

#=>
We need to buy Cheese today.
We need to buy Milk today.
We need to buy Bread today.
fig08.rb:4:in `readline': end of file reached (EOFError)
    from fig08.rb:4:in `<main>'
```

You will notice that we didn't correctly rescue and handle the EOFError that Ruby raised when we tried to reach beyond the end of the file. We could correctly handle this by rescuing the error and closing the file.

```ruby
#!/usr/bin/env ruby
begin
  file = File.open("shopping_list.txt","r")
  while(item = file.readline) != nil
    puts "We need to buy #{item.chomp} today."
  end
rescue EOFError
  file.close
end

#=>
We need to buy Cheese today.
We need to buy Milk today.
We need to buy Bread today.
```

We can also adjust our file pointers location if required; if we read all or part of the file's contents, but then need to re-read this again, we can use the rewind method to adjust the file pointer back to the beginning of the file.

```ruby
#!/usr/bin/env ruby
file = File.open("shopping_list.txt", "r")
puts file.readline.chomp
file.rewind
puts file.readline.chomp
file.close
#=>
Cheese
Cheese
```

Likewise, we can seek forward rather than rewind backward within a file pointer; we simply specify the byte that we want to skip to, and our file pointer is moved.

Our input file:

```
Testing
Hello
Abc
123456
```

```ruby
#!/usr/bin/env ruby
file = File.open("fig13.txt", "r")
puts file.readline.chomp
file.seek(20, IO::SEEK_SET)
puts file.readline.chomp
file.close
```

```
#=>
Testing
3456
```

Seek Types

Previously, we used the IO::SEEK_SET constant that defines where to seek to given the number of bytes as the initial parameter; there are three seek types that can be used

Seek Type	Details
IO::SEEK_SET	Seeks to the absolute location given by first integer number parameter from the start of the file
IO::SEEK_CUR	Seeks to first integer number parameter plus current position (i.e., seeks X number of bytes from the current position)
IO::SEEK_END	Seeks to first integer number parameter plus end of stream (i.e., seeks from the end of the file, so seeking a negative number allows rewinding by a number of bytes)

File Modes

You will notice so far that we have used the mode r when dealing with opening and reading a file; this mode stands for read-only, which simply allows our file to be read, but nothing can be written to the file handle.

Mode	Details
R	Read-only, starting at beginning of file (default)
r+	Read-write, starts at beginning of file
W	Write-only, truncates existing file to an empty file, or creates a new file if it doesn't already exist
w+	Read-write, truncates existing file to an empty file, or creates a new file if it doesn't already exist
A	Write-only, each write call appends data at end of file. Creates a new file for writing if file does not exist
a+	Read-write, each write call appends data at end of file. Creates a new file for reading and writing if file does not exist

We will now use other methods of opening files to write/append to files, rather than just reading data from a file; this could be used for writing log files, reading a file for validation, then appending a reject message against each line if required.

```ruby
#!/usr/bin/env ruby
file = File.open("test4.txt", "w")
file.puts "Hello Matt!"
file.close
```

And a file named test4.txt has been created as follows:

```
Hello Matt!
```

Running the code again will simply truncate the file to an empty file, and write the same line again, so our output file will always contain the same content; we could switch the file open mode from Write to Append as follows, then run the code three times in a row

```ruby
#!/usr/bin/env ruby
file = File.open("test-append.txt", "a")
file.puts "Hello there!"
file.close
```

And the output file contents, once we have run the code three times:

```
Hello there!
Hello there!
Hello there!
```

Network Input/Output

While we have mainly detailed File Input/Output, similar functionality exists for dealing with Network Input/Output using the BasicSocket class (a subclass of the IO class). There are also a number of specialized classes such as TCPSocket (for dealing with TCP connections), UDPSocket (for dealing with UDP connections), and many more.

For our first example, we can use the TCPSocket to open a simple telnet session to an external service, such as the Blinken Lights ASCII Starwars via telnet service: (http://www.blinkenlights.nl/services.html#starwars)

```ruby
#!/usr/bin/env ruby
require 'socket'

socket = TCPSocket.open("towel.blinkenlights.nl", 23)

while line = socket.gets
  puts line.chop
end
socket.close
```

```
8888888888  888      88888
    88      88  88 88  88  88
  8888  88  88    88  88888
      88 88 88888888 88    88
88888888  88 88      88 88      888888

    88  88  88    888      88888      888888
    88  88  88  88 88      88  88  88
    88 8888 88 88    88  88888      8888
      888  888 88888888 88    88      88
        88  88  88      88 88    8888888
```

We can take this further by creating a Server and a Client, and make these two applications talk to each other.

Server:

```ruby
#!/usr/bin/env ruby
require 'socket'
BasicSocket.do_not_reverse_lookup = true
client = UDPSocket.new
client.bind('0.0.0.0', 33333)
data, address = client.recvfrom(1024)
puts "#{address} says: #{data}"
client.close
```

Client:

```ruby
#!/usr/bin/env ruby
require 'socket'
sock = UDPSocket.new
data = gets
sock.send(data, 0, '127.0.0.1', 33333)
sock.close
```

We then run the Server, and the Client at the same time; the Server opens a socket ready for a client to connect. Running the Client requests user input, which when submitted uses the UDPSocket to pass data over to the server that outputs the message before exiting.

Client:

Hello there server!

Server:

["AF_INET", 52465, "127.0.0.1", "127.0.0.1"] says: Hello there server

Higher Level Network Input/Output

Although we have used the BasicSocket in the previous examples, along with their subclasses such as TCPSocket and UDPSocket, these are low-level network Input/Outputs and require very complex code to retrieve simple data. We can instead use some higher-level libraries, such as the net library that allows access to network resources, such as HTTP commonly used for websites. For this example we connect to a website, and initially check that we receive an OK status back (an HTTP 200 code, meaning that page is responding), and we then search or scan through the source code looking for the source within any HTML image tags, and display these on the screen

```ruby
#!/usr/bin/env ruby
require 'net/http'

conn = Net::HTTP.get_response('www.mattclements.co.uk', '/')
if conn.message == 'OK'
  conn.body.scan(/<img src="(.*?)"/) { |image| puts image }
end

#=>
/content/images/2014/Jul/avatar.jpg
```

CHAPTER 15

■ ■ ■

Files and Directories

Continuing from the previous chapter, here we look at Ruby's ability to deal with files and directories. Within a Ruby application, we may need to open files, amend those files, and write them back to a particular directory, or we may need to open a file, process this file, and move the file into another directory.

To do this we will use the File class, used in the previous chapter, along with the Dir class which is Ruby's method of interpreting and interacting with directory paths. Many of the methods of this class have names similar to the relevant Linux command.

To start with, we can begin navigating through the hosts file system, and printing out the current directory at each stage, as with the below example we can also change directory within a block, which will revert to the previous directory once the block has finished being executed.

```ruby
#!/usr/bin/env ruby
Dir.chdir("/var/log")
puts Dir.pwd

Dir.chdir("/tmp") do
    puts Dir.pwd
  Dir.chdir("/Users/matt") do
    puts Dir.pwd
  end
  puts Dir.pwd
end
puts Dir.pwd

#=>
/var/log
/tmp
/Users/matt
/tmp
/var/log
```

This is particularly useful when you need to read and write a file within a particular location, the block can navigate you to a particular directory to read/write files, and once completed will change back to the previous directory automatically without you having to store and change back to the initial directory. chdir stands for change directory and is similar to the cd command within Unix applications. The pwd method stands for print working directory, which shares the same name as the Unix command. The pwd method is actually an alias for the getwd method and either can be used.

Now that we can navigate to various directories, and return the path to the current directory, we can take this further by outputting a list of files/directories within our current working directory. To do so we can use the entries method, which is similar to the ls command within Unix. Using this method returns an array of all files and directories within the current working directory. We can also pass over an optional second parameter as the encoding of the directory, if this is not passed in, then the filesystem encoding is used.

```
#!/usr/bin/env ruby
Dir.chdir("/Users/matt/Projects/ruby_book") do
  puts Dir.pwd
  puts Dir.entries('.').inspect
end
#=>
[".", "..", ".editorconfig", ".git", ".gitignore", "ch03", "ch04", "ch05",
"ch06", "ch07", "ch08", "ch09", "ch12", "ch13", "ch14", "ch15"]
```

This example shows a few things worth investigating further. The Dir.entries() method accepts a directory as its first parameter. As we have already changed our working directory to the folder for which we would like to list the files and directories, we can simply use '.' as the directory. This stands for the current directory. Also within our list of files, we can see files named "." and ".." this is Unix's way of showing that we can navigate to the current directory (".") and the parent directory (".."), the other files/directories are then listed, ".editorconfig" is a file, "ch03" is a directory. We can compare this to the output of an ls command in Unix that shows a number of similarities.

```
ls -a
.               .gitignore    ch06         ch12
..              ch03          ch07         ch13
.editorconfig   ch04          ch08         ch14
.git            ch05          ch09         ch15
```

We can use a method within Ruby's Dir class called exist? to check the existence of a directory. Note that this method strictly checks that the path provided exists and is a directory. Calling this method with a file rather than a directory will return false.

```
#!/usr/bin/env ruby
Dir.chdir("/Users/matt/Projects/ruby_book") do
  puts Dir.exists?('ch15')
  puts Dir.exists?('ch15/fig02.rb')
end
```

```
#=>
true
false
```

We have the option to output the home directory of either the current user, or another user, if we pass the username in as a parameter.

```
#!/usr/bin/env ruby
puts Dir.home()
puts Dir.home("root")
#=>
/Users/matt
/var/root
```

We can also chroot within our Ruby application. A chroot changes the current processes view on the filesystem to only include the directory supplied and all child directories, but will not allow access to other directories above. We must also run any process that uses the chroot method under a privileged user such as running the code with the sudo command.

```
#!/usr/bin/env ruby
Dir.chdir("/var")
puts Dir.pwd
puts Dir.entries('.').inspect

Dir.chroot("/var")
Dir.chdir("/")
puts Dir.pwd
puts Dir.entries('.').inspect

Dir.chdir("/etc")
puts Dir.pwd

#=>
```

sudo ruby fig05.rb   • • • • • • • • • • •

```
/var
[".", "..", "agentx", "at", "audit", "backups", "db", "empty", "folders",
"jabberd", "lib", "log", "mail", "msgs", "netboot", "networkd", "root",
"rpc", "run", "rwho", "spool", "tmp", "vm", "yp"]

/
[".", "..", "agentx", "at", "audit", "backups", "db", "empty", "folders",
"jabberd", "lib", "log", "mail", "msgs", "netboot", "networkd", "root",
"rpc", "run", "rwho", "spool", "tmp", "vm", "yp"]

fig05.rb:11:in `chdir': No such file or directory @ dir_chdir - /etc
(Errno::ENOENT)
        from fig05.rb:11:in `<main>'
```

You will notice that we list the contents of the /var directory, we then lock the process to the /var directory, and output the contents of the root of our (chrooted) filesystem, which is actually the /var directory. When we then attempt to change to the /etc directory (which does exist on our full filesystem) this cannot be found as the process is looking within the chrooted file system. Therefore when changing to the /etc directory, we are actually attempting to change to the /var/etc directory instead.

We can use the Ruby each and foreach methods to loop through the directory listings, similar to the entries method, which returns an array of all entries.

```
#!/usr/bin/env ruby
Dir.foreach(".") {|f| puts "Found #{f}" }

puts

directory = Dir.new(".")
directory.each  {|f| puts "Found #{f}" }
#=>
Found .
Found ..
Found fig01.rb
Found fig02.rb

Found .
Found ..
Found fig01.rb
Found fig02.rb
```

The final method that we cover here is the Dir.glob method, which is one of the more advanced topics that we will cover during this chapter. A glob is a pattern match for filenames, we pass in a pattern as an array or a string, and the method returns matching results. This is often assumed as a regular expression, which is not the case; this is more similar to a shell filename glob such as:

```
ls *.rb
```

The preceding is a Unix command to list all files that contain "(anything).rb" as the filename.

```
#!/usr/bin/env ruby
puts Dir.glob("fig01.??").inspect
puts Dir.glob("*.[a-z][a-z]").inspect
puts Dir.glob("*.{rb}").inspect
puts Dir.glob("*").inspect
```

```
#=>
["fig01.rb"]
["fig01.rb", "fig02.rb", "fig03.rb", "fig04.rb", "fig05.rb", "fig06.rb",
"fig07.rb", "fig08.rb", "fig09.rb", "fig10.rb"]
["fig01.rb", "fig02.rb", "fig03.rb", "fig04.rb", "fig05.rb", "fig06.rb",
"fig07.rb", "fig08.rb", "fig09.rb", "fig10.rb"]
["fig01.rb", "fig02.rb", "fig03.rb", "fig04.rb", "fig05.rb", "fig06.rb",
"fig07.rb", "fig08.rb", "fig09.rb", "fig10.rb", "testing", "testing2",
"testing3", "testing5"]
```

You will notice various patterns in the preceding code that start to demonstrate some of the functionality of globbing, the first example, lists all files that are named fig01.(Any Character)(Any Character).

Table 15-1. *Glob Characters*

Glob Character	Examples	Details
*		Matches any file. Can be restricted with other values either side of the * character
	c*	Matches files beginning with a c
	*c	Matches files ending with a c
	c	Matches files with a c in them (including beginning or end)
**		Matches recursive directories (directories within directories)
?		Matches any 1 character (i.e., the letter c)
[set]	[a-z]	Matches any 1 character within the set, exactly as with a Regular Expression. The example here is any character that is between a and z, but we could change this to [^a-z], which is any character not between a and z.
{a,b}		Matches any 1 character listed, the example would be a single character that is either a or b.
\		Escapes a metacharacter. For example if we were looking for a filename that contained the * symbol, we could use *** meaning contains the * character somewhere within the filename.

Directory Modification

Previously, we have been using the Ruby Dir class to look, navigate, and interrogate our filesystems, we can now begin to modify the filesystem's directories.

To start with, we will use the mkdir method, which creates a directory (in similar fashion to the mkdir command within Unix operating systems). A SystemCallError is raised if the directory cannot be created (for example, due to a privilege issue).

```ruby
#!/usr/bin/env ruby
puts Dir.pwd
Dir.mkdir("testing")
Dir.chdir("testing")
puts Dir.pwd

#=>
/Users/matt/Projects/ruby_book/ch15
/Users/matt/Projects/ruby_book/ch15/testing
```

We can pass a second parameter to the mkdir method, which is for the new permissions of the directory using the File::umask value (0777 for read/write/execute to the owner, the owners group, and all other users; 0000 for no access to any user at all).

```ruby
#!/usr/bin/env ruby
Dir.mkdir("testing2",0600)
Dir.mkdir("testing3",0755)

#=>
ls -la
drw-------  2 matt  staff   68 14 Oct 18:32 testing2
drwxr-xr-x  2 matt  staff   68 14 Oct 18:32 testing3
```

We can also delete folders, which will raise a subclass of SystemCallError if the directory is not empty. To delete a folder we can use the delete, rmdir, or unlink method which are all identical in the code that they execute.

```ruby
 #!/usr/bin/env ruby
Dir.delete("testing4")
Dir.delete("testing5")
#=>
fig08.rb:3:in `delete': Directory not empty @ dir_s_rmdir - testing5
(Errno::ENOTEMPTY)
     from fig08.rb:3:in `<main>'
```

File Access

In the previous chapter we covered the File class in regards to the Input/Output functionalities within Ruby. We will extend this further during this chapter, by outlining some additional methods within the File class that we have not used previously.

First, we will look at viewing the meta-data available on a file, initially looking at the Dates and Times that files were created, last modified, and last accessed (note that these are ISO formatted dates).

```
#!/usr/bin/env ruby
puts File.ctime('fig01.rb')
puts File.mtime('fig01.rb')
puts File.atime('fig01.rb')
#=>
2014-10-14 17:42:26 +0100
2014-10-14 17:42:52 +0100
2014-10-14 17:42:26 +0100
```

We can also modify both the access and modification times if we want to:

```
#!/usr/bin/env ruby
puts File.mtime('fig01.rb')
puts File.atime('fig01.rb')
File.utime(Time.new('2020','01','01','00','00','00','+01:00'),
Time.new('1990','06','14','06','23','11','+01:00'),'fig01.rb')
puts File.mtime('fig01.rb')
puts File.atime('fig01.rb')
#=>
2014-10-14 17:42:52 +0100
2014-10-14 17:42:26 +0100
1990-06-14 06:23:11 +0100
2019-12-31 23:00:00 +0000
```

Notice that Ruby has handled the change in time zones for us also, we set the access time to 01/01/2020 at midnight at 1 hour ahead of UTC time, however as December in the UK is actually at +0 hours ahead of UTC this has been changed to 11p.m. the night before. These dates and times have been modified at filesystem level.

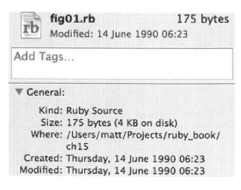

125

```
#!/usr/bin/env ruby
file = File.open("test-append.txt", "a")
file.puts "Hello there!"
file.close
```

Like with our exist? method within the Dir class, we have a similar method within the File class. This method checks whether the file exists, however does not provide the additional check (like the Dir class did) that the file is not actually a directory. Instead we can use the file? method to check that the file is not actually a directory.

```
#!/usr/bin/env ruby
puts File.exists?('fig01.rb')
puts File.exists?('testing')

puts File.file?('fig01.rb')
puts File.file?('testing')

#=>
true
true
true
false
```

We can integrate various details regarding the file, such as the file's actual name (rather than the path to the file that we are looking for), we can return the extension name (txt for a Text File, rb for Ruby source code), the directory path for the file that we are looking at, and whether the file is empty (zero bytes).

```
#!/usr/bin/env ruby
puts File.basename("/Users/matt/Projects/ruby_book/ch15/fig01.rb")
puts File.extname("/Users/matt/Projects/ruby_book/ch15/fig01.rb")
puts File.dirname("/Users/matt/Projects/ruby_book/ch15/fig01.rb")
puts File.zero?("/Users/matt/Projects/ruby_book/ch15/fig01.rb")
#=>
fig01.rb
.rb
/Users/matt/Projects/ruby_book/ch15
false
```

File Modification

Finally we will cover the modification of files. We have previously dealt with the access and modification of directories using the Dir class followed by the access of files by the File class.

We can rename files within Ruby using the File.rename method, supplying the initial filename, and the destination filename:

```
#!/usr/bin/env ruby
File.rename("test.txt", "test2.txt")
```

We can also symbolically link (often called a soft-link) files using the File.symlink method

```
#!/usr/bin/env ruby
File.symlink("test2.txt", "test.txt")
```

Running an ls -l command in Unix now shows the link.

```
lrwxr-xr-x  1 matt  staff    9 15 Oct 13:55 test.txt -> test2.txt
-rw-r--r--  1 matt  staff    0 15 Oct 13:51 test2.txt
```

We also can truncate a file to either 0 bytes (an empty file), or trim down the file to be a certain number of bytes. To do so, we use the File.truncate method, passing in the filename as the initial parameter, and the number of bytes as the second parameter.

```
#!/usr/bin/env ruby
puts File.size("test2.txt")
File.truncate("test2.txt",6)
puts File.size("test2.txt")
File.truncate("test2.txt",0)
puts File.size("test2.txt")
#=>
10
6
0
```

CHAPTER 16

■ ■ ■

Metaprogramming

Metaprogramming is the ability to write code that operates on other code, rather than data. In all previous chapters we have written code that operates on other data, such as the reading/writing of variables, outputting to screen, communicating with files or other input output streams. Metaprogramming is the ability to write code that adjusts the functionality of a class or dynamically call a method without a direct call to this method existing within the executable code. This is extremely useful when you want to amend the method being called depending on a scenario, or if you want to modify the behavior of a class during the runtime.

Metaprogramming exists within most object-oriented programming languages, but often is not a frequently used feature, or one that is not well documented. Some other examples are

- Lisp (Homoiconicity)
- Java (Reflection)
- C# (Reflection)

Classes

For example, we want to amend the Ruby's Array class to perform some mathematical equations, and return the value. We simply "redefine" the Array class with an additional method, and then call this to see the results:

```
#!/usr/bin/env ruby
class Array
  def maths(method)
    inject {|result, i| result ? result.send(method, i) : i }
  end
end

puts [1000.0, 200.0, 50.0].maths("/")

puts [10, 2].maths("*")

puts [10, 2].maths("+")
```

```
#=>
0.1
20
12
```

Likewise, the String class cannot split a string into sentences; we can simply add an additional method to allow us to action this.

```ruby
#!/usr/bin/env ruby
class String
  def sentence
    return self.split('.')
  end
end
```

```ruby
puts "Lorem ipsum dolor sit amet, consectetur adipisicing elit, sed do
eiusmod tempor incididunt ut labore et dolore magna aliqua. Ut enim ad
minim veniam, quis nostrud exercitation ullamco laboris nisi ut aliquip ex
ea commodo consequat. Duis aute irure dolor in reprehenderit in voluptate
velit esse cillum dolore eu fugiat nulla pariatur. Excepteur sint occaecat
cupidatat non proident, sunt in culpa qui officia deserunt mollit anim id
est laborum.".sentence.inspect
```

```
#=>
["Lorem ipsum dolor sit amet, consectetur adipisicing elit, sed do eiusmod
tempor incididunt ut labore et dolore magna aliqua", " Ut enim ad minim
veniam, quis nostrud exercitation ullamco laboris nisi ut aliquip ex ea
commodo consequat", " Duis aute irure dolor in reprehenderit in voluptate
velit esse cillum dolore eu fugiat nulla pariatur", " Excepteur sint
occaecat cupidatat non proident, sunt in culpa qui officia deserunt mollit
anim id est laborum"]
```

Here, we added the sentence method to the String class, then ran the sentence method on a string that contained a paragraph of Lorem Ipsum text. When we executed the code, we were returned, and output the contents of this paragraph split into sentences (or rather by splitting the paragraph where a full stop was found).

A word of caution at this point however, Ruby operates an Open Class approach using metaprogramming, meaning you can define and refine methods as much as you want; while this can be incredibly useful, this lets you overwrite initial methods within Ruby-based classes, which may impact something else that your application is doing.

```ruby
#!/usr/bin/env ruby

puts "123456789".length

class String
  def length
    return 100
  end
end

puts "123456789".length
#=>
9
100
```

While this is an obvious example, the two calls to length could be in separate parts of our Ruby application, which would suddenly start performing in an odd way, without any indication that metaprogramming was to blame. We can, however, use the methods method that informs us of the methods that are available for an Object of a certain class. The output that follows has been cut down to show the differences between the initial call and the second call.

```ruby
#!/usr/bin/env ruby

puts "123456789".methods.inspect

class String
  def my_new_method
    return 100
  end
end

puts "123456789".methods.inspect
#=>
[]
[:my_new_method]
```

Method Calls

We can also dynamically call a method by using Ruby's call method. This allows a method to be dynamically called rather than being statically programmed to make a call to the method. For example:

```ruby
#!/usr/bin/env ruby
puts "A,B,C,D,E,F".split(',')
puts "A,B,C,D,E,F".method("split").call(',')
#=>
```

```
A
B
C
D
E
F
A
B
C
D
E
F
```

In the first example, we used the actual split method that exists within the Ruby String class, whereas in the second example we dynamically called the split method on the String, passing in the parameter required to split. While this does not seem extremely useful when being written statically as in the preceding we could for example, retrieve the method calls from a database or file, and execute the code retrieved dynamically; or we could dynamically run code supplied by the user.

```ruby
#!/usr/bin/env ruby
def output(object,method,params)
    puts object.method(method).call(params)
end

output "A,B,C,D", 'split', ','

#=>
A
B
C
D
```

We can also write our code to dynamically accept various method calls, without previously defining the method within our application. For example, we want to write a validation class, where we can check a user's input against a list of values that are allowed. We could write some static code to check these values against a static list as follows:

```ruby
#!/usr/bin/env ruby
class Validation
    def validate_pet(value)
        return ['Cat', 'Dog', 'Bird'].include? value
    end
end

validator = Validation.new
puts validator.validate_pet 'Dog'
puts validator.validate_pet 'Rat'
```

```
#=>
true
false
```

However, whenever we want to change the allowed list of pets we need to modify the initial Validation class; likewise this code is not re-usable if we simply want to check our value against a list of allowed values. Instead, we can use metaprogramming to dynamically call methods without them being predefined.

```ruby
#!/usr/bin/env ruby
class Validation
    attr_accessor :value

    def initialize(value)
        @value = value
    end

    CHECK_QUERY_REGEX = /^is_((?:_or_)?[a-z]+?)+\?$/i

    def method_missing(meth, *args, &block)
        if CHECK_QUERY_REGEX.match meth.to_s
          self.class.class_eval <<-end_eval
            def #{meth}
              self.__send__ :check_value, "#{meth}"
            end
          end_eval
          self.__send__(meth, *args, &block)
        else
          super
        end
    end

    private
      def check_value(query)
          allowed_values = query[3..-2].split("_or_")
          allowed_values.any? { |s| s == @value }
      end
end

animal = Validation.new("dog")
puts animal.is_cat?
puts animal.is_dog?
puts animal.is_cat_or_dog?

vehicle = Validation.new("car")
puts vehicle.is_van?
puts vehicle.is_van_or_car_or_motorbike?
```

```
#=>
false
true
true
false
true
```

The preceding example is a complex example; however we can step through this in sections, beginning with the initialize of a new object of our Validation class:

```
class Validation
    attr_accessor :value

    def initialize(value)
        @value = value
    end
...
end
```

This section simply sets an instance variable (@value) that can be accessed (read/written to) by our class. This allows our constructor method to have a value passed to it, which is stored within the object for further processing.

```
CHECK_QUERY_REGEX = /^is_((?:_or_)?[a-z]+?)+\?$/i
```

This is a regular expression that simply checks against the pattern is_x? or is_x_or_y? or is_x_or_y_or_z?, and so on.

```
class Validation
...
    def method_missing(meth, *args, &block)
        if CHECK_QUERY_REGEX.match meth.to_s
          self.class.class_eval <<-end_eval
            def #{meth}
              self.__send__ :check_value, "#{meth}"
            end
          end_eval
          self.__send__(meth, *args, &block)
        else
          super
        end
    end
...
end
```

The method_missing method within Ruby is a special method. This method handles whenever a method is requested that does not exist within the class. The method_missing method accepts three variables: the method itself being called, the arguments supplied, and finally the block that the method was called from. If we don't want to handle this method, we simply call super, which raises a method_missing exception, rather than handling it. Within the preceding example, we check the method name against our regular expression; if the method name is in the format that we require, then we handle this method, otherwise we simply call super. On handling the method we call the check_value method with the method name requested as our parameter (for example is_dog_or_cat?)

```
class Validation
  .
    private
      def check_value(query)
          allowed_values = query[3..-2].split("_or_")
          allowed_values.any? { |s| s == @value }
      end
end
```

Finally, we define a private method name check_value that accepts the method name initially called as its parameter. We split up the method name by removing the is_ and ? at either end, followed by splitting the remaining string (dog_or_cat) into an array where the string contains the _or_ characters. We then check this array (which contains dog and cat) against our initial instance variable to see if the String we are checking is contained in the method name called.

This is highly useful, as we have now written some *dry* (don't repeat yourself) code that can be easily implemented whenever we want to check a value against a predefined list of allowed values. This could be used to check Countries, County/States, or any other number of predefined lists of values.

Index

Get the eBook for only $10!

Now you can take the weightless companion with you anywhere, anytime. Your purchase of this book entitles you to 3 electronic versions for only $10.

This Apress title will prove so indispensible that you'll want to carry it with you everywhere, which is why we are offering the eBook in 3 formats for only $10 if you have already purchased the print book.

Convenient and fully searchable, the PDF version enables you to easily find and copy code—or perform examples by quickly toggling between instructions and   applications. The MOBI format is ideal for your Kindle, while the ePUB can be utilized on a variety of mobile devices.

Go to www.apress.com/promo/tendollars to purchase your companion eBook.